Successful College Application Strategies for Truly Exceptional Individuals

How to Make Ivy League and Elite Colleges Compete for YOU

2nd Edition

Daniel Farber Huang

Successful College Application Strategies for Truly Exceptional Individuals

How to Make Ivy League and Elite Colleges Compete for YOU

2025 Edition

©2025 Daniel Farber Huang

All Rights Reserved.

No part of this book shall be reproduced or transmitted in any form or by any means, electronic, mechanical, magnetic, and photographic, including photocopying, recording, or by any information storage and retrieval system, without prior written permission of the publisher.

No patent liability is assumed with respect to the use of the information contained herein. Although every precaution has been taken in the preparation of this book, the publisher and author assume no responsibility for errors or omissions. Neither is any liability assumed for damages resulting from the use of the information contained herein.

Published by Princeton Studios

The Reviews Are In!

Selected by Kirkus Reviews as an Editor's Choice book

"A wise and easy-to-read manual for thriving in Ivy League admissions and beyond."

"Huang presents a how-to guide for college-bound students applying to Ivy League schools.

From the introduction, the author makes it clear that his book is aimed at prospective university students who wish to "present themselves in their best, most brilliant light without coming across as egotistical, entitled, or just unpleasant to be around." In a separate letter to parents, he notes that the Ivy League schools aren't a good fit for everyone, and that he won't be providing the typical recommendations for extracurriculars and AP classes that other guides do. What Huang offers instead is the perspective of an admission reader—the "tired, overworked, bleary-eyed" person speed-reading through the digital records of thousands of students. Given the nature of modern-day admissions, he advises teens to start early by developing their "personal brand," ensuring that their actions and choices reflect the persona they wish to convey in essays, resumes, and recommendation letters.

In the book's second section, Huang breaks down his advice into easily applicable "tactics, techniques, and procedures." Throughout, his tone is honest, sometimes hard-nosed, and intended for the student (or parent) who wants to understand how the process really works. Huang offers personal anecdotes about former clients he's helped, including a student who applied to the top 17 schools in the United States and had to create a spreadsheet to keep track of the 57 supplemental essays that had to be written as a result: "We identified 13 major themes, and then sorted the 57 essays into their respective themes....In several cases we were able to reduce, reuse, and recycle."

This focus on direct, practical advice, taken from experience, effectively extends beyond the college application process. Reflecting on the benefits of having a job as a teenager, he advises, "If you are working at a retail store, pay attention to how it runs so you could be qualified to manage the store, don't just clock in and clock out." In the end, the book not only prepares one for acceptance into top colleges, but also provides tools for succeeding in the larger world.

A wise and easy-to-read manual for thriving in Ivy League admissions and beyond."

Source: https://www.kirkusreviews.com/book-reviews/daniel-farber-huang/successful-college-application-strategies-for-trul/

This book is dedicated to
the glorious, courageous, one and only You.

About the Author and EchoStream Talent Group

Daniel Farber Huang, founder of EchoStream Talent Group, is an internationally recognized expert in college admissions strategy and high-stakes achievement advising. A former admissions reader for the University of Pennsylvania and a Harvard-educated journalist, Daniel has helped guide students into the world's most selective universities — including Stanford, Yale, Oxford, MIT, and the Ivy Leagues.

At EchoStream, Daniel leads a multidisciplinary team of strategists and specialists who work with extraordinary students, families, and professionals. The firm offers a discreet, high-touch consulting model that combines deep editorial expertise, elite institutional knowledge, and an unmatched commitment to client outcomes.

While EchoStream operates as a full-service advisory group, Daniel remains personally involved with a select group of clients who seek not just application support, but a long-term strategic partner in defining and achieving bold academic and professional goals.

Read his latest insights and thought leadership at:

www.echostreamgroup.com

For consultations, inquiries, or speaking engagements:

info@echostreamgroup.com

At EchoStream Talent Group, we don't help students fit in, we help them stand out.

Table of Contents

Topic	Page
Introduction	i
Section 1 – What to watch out for	**1**
Chapter 1 – The practical reality	1
Chapter 2 – The Tao of Applications	9
Section 2 – Tactics, Techniques and Procedures	**13**
Chapter 3 – Tactics, Techniques, Procedures	17
Chapter 4 – Tactics	19
Chapter 5 – Know thyself	29
Chapter 6 – Lead with Humility (i.e., Don't be an Ass)	33
Chapter 7 – Treat Your Application Process Like a Job	35
Chapter 8 – Become Subject Matter Knowledgeable	41
Chapter 9 – Impersonate an Adult	49
Chapter 10 – Advocate for Yourself	53
Chapter 11 – Advocate for Others	61
Chapter 12 – Create Information and Generate Deliverables	65
Chapter 13 – Develop Your Personal Brand	109
Chapter 14 – Learn how to Tell Your Story	117
Chapter 15 – Practice Frequent Self-Care	123
Epilogue	129
APPENDIX	131
Prospective Media Outlets for Articles	133
About the Author	139
Bibliography	141

Introduction

Dear High Schoolers thinking about elite colleges –

I'll state right at the start that the recommendations in this book aren't for everyone. And probably won't work for everyone. And that's the point actually.

The goal here is to help a handful of candidates employ specific tactics and strategies that will help them distinguish themselves positively among playing fields of tens of thousands of other elite college applicants.

This book will help a select few people be recognized as absurdly unique, talented, and promising. This book is for the bright, the brave, and the bold (i.e., YOU).

I'll leave the recommended test taking, grades, sports and extracurriculars to other books. You've already read them. The practical techniques in this book go far beyond what most other advisors are doing and recommending. Those books tell you how to make a hamburger, this book tells you how to create your special sauce that makes you the one every school wants.

Since you chose to open up this book, I know you already know that every year hundreds of thousands of high school juniors apply to the top colleges and universities for admission into the incoming freshman class. At the most competitive schools, the majority of applicants are perfectly qualified to attend, but only a minute few are made an offer.

When I say "qualified" applicants, I am referring to hardworking, hopeful students who have made sure they earned the acceptable grades, test scores, AP courses, activities, recommendations, and other elements that meet or exceed the profile of a school's accepted applicant pool.

The monumental challenge for any qualified applicant is to distinguish themselves and stand out in a massively overpacked, high performing playing field. This book is specifically written for people who are willing to be bold and courageous to present themselves in their best, most brilliant light without coming across as egotistical, entitled, or just unpleasant to be around. The ultimate goal for any reader who employs the strategies here is to not only receive one offer letter from a top school, but several offers to pick and choose from.

Let me preface everything that follows by saying I've advised both undergraduate and graduate school applicants on how best to position themselves and tell their stories, charging clients anywhere from pro bono to $1,000 per hour depending on their parent's ability to pay and how much I liked working with them. On balance, my clients have consistently been accepted to their top school choices, and often obtained acceptance offers from multiple schools. The actionable steps that are explained here are the same ones I have coached my student clients to take, with consistent and exceptional success over the last several years.

I'm a father of 4 children, who have attended Dartmouth, Stanford, Georgetown, and a trade school. I went to New York University for undergrad, got my MBA from U Penn, Wharton, and a second Masters in Journalism from Harvard Extension School. My spouse attended Dartmouth (BA), UPenn (MBA), Johns Hopkins (MA), George Washington (MPH) [3 Masters degrees], and University of Illinois – Chicago (DrPH). I've written books, published articles and Op-Eds and am an active writer. I have disparate corporate work experience (ranging from investment banker to consultant to private company CEO), and was also an MBA admissions reviewer for a couple of years to a Top 3 business school (the rank changes year by year). In short, I've leveraged my real-world life experiences to advise my clients on the best ways to make themselves interesting and distinctive, show what they have and can continue to accomplish, craft powerful narratives, and shine in the eyes of overworked, slightly cynical, bleary-eyed admissions committees.

If you are open-minded about pushing your proverbial boundaries beyond what you ever imagined you could be capable of, this book is for you. People whom I have helped have gotten into not only their dream schools but also other solid options by having distinguished themselves in any number of significant ways, including:

- Developing genuine subject matter knowledge worthy of leading adults in their field;
- Teaching formal workshops and classes on their areas of subject matter knowledge;
- Giving major talks and presentations, including multiple TEDx Talks;
- Publishing numerous articles and Op-Eds in respected newspapers, magazines, and online platforms;
- Exhibiting in solo and group shows at museums and galleries;
- Getting hired into highly competitive or custom-designed internships;
- Establishing and leading not-for-profit entities that make a real impact;
- Being invited to join editorial boards of respected publications; and
- Taking leadership roles and Board seats in established organizations and societies.

In my private consultations – and now throughout this book – I tell my clients that applying to serious colleges is a serious endeavor and I'm not interested in wasting your time. Even more importantly, I'm not interested in wasting my time. So here's my promise: I will speak to you clearly and directly, without a lot of fluff or platitudes and get right to the point. I will present information to you as one adult to another. I will advise, counsel, and guide you but I'm not going to baby or hand-hold you, because you don't need me to. If you do, this book isn't right for you.

To put my approach in context, I genuinely enjoy working with students and helping them succeed wildly. There have been some instances where I have had to fire some clients (politely, of course) because they were perhaps too entitled by their parents, too overconfident about how amazing they were, or just lazy about their own aspirations. It wasn't a good use of my time.

There have been a small number of situations where it was clear the student was being forced by their parent to work with someone like me but actually did not want to attend college. After it became clear their heart wasn't in it (college, that is), I've counseled those high schoolers to have a sincere conversation with their parents and make their true feelings known. I would much rather they redirect their efforts so they can pursue their true personal goals. I would rather help a student not go to college than go where they don't want to be. Believe it or not, you have decades ahead of you to map out your life. You don't have to rush just because everyone around you is doing so.

One final note: Many of the strategies and procedures I discuss herein are written with the starting assumption that you are already meaningfully capable and competent in whatever areas of interest you are seeking to elevate and enhance. For example, when I give practical advice on How to Get Published, I am assuming you already know how to write well enough that your craft is publication worthy. Or if you're not that skilled yet but aspire to be, I am assuming you are already making concerted efforts to hone your craft on your own. You already have done your own research into the abundance of resources available online that can refine your desired skills and are already taking advantage of those learning opportunities. I'm not here to teach you how to write, I'm here to get you past the gatekeepers so you can show the decision makers what you're genuinely capable of.

Dear Parents of the high school student who picked up this book –

If you are reading this, you're concerned about your child's chances of getting accepted into their (or your) top school choice(s). I get it. I've been there many times myself as a parent.

In this guidebook, I discuss what has worked for my students, my own children, and me as we have worked through their college application journeys from drafting to submission and ultimately to acceptance offers received. We will look at the Practical and Philosophical aspects as well as the vital Bigger Picture approach to successful college applications.

If you want to help your child succeed with the tactics in this book, I recommend that you keep an open mind and be flexible to accommodate and support your child as they pursue outsized goals. One of my goals with my students is to help set them on a steeper, more meaningful upward trajectory toward their interests and aspirations. I advise my students that the strategies we are pursuing are not merely for college admissions, rather they are big reaches that will help propel them toward their larger life goals during college and beyond.

Sound confusing? It is, I know. But we'll make progress fast if you're willing to.

Be aware that neither this book nor I am here to hand-hold your child. Our goal is to light the dark and confusing path ahead so they can be bold and take bigger, longer strides toward achieving highly distinctive and impressive goals beyond what they thought they were capable of achieving on their own.

Section 1 – What to watch out for

Table of Contents

Topic	Page

Chapter 1 – The practical reality 1
   The Practical 1
      Start early 1
      Forget "passion" 2
      Pull, don't push 3
      Emulate 4
      Understand the process 4
   What matters most in an application? 5
      Essays 6
      Resumés 6
         Not Student Clubs 7
      Recommendations 7

Chapter 2 – The Tao of Applications 9
      Intrinsic versus extrinsic values 9
      It's only four years 10
   The Worst Advice for High School Students I Have Ever Heard 11

Chapter 1 – The practical reality

Think bigger than college.

There's Harvard, Princeton, Dartmouth, Columbia, and the others that make up the Ivy League. There's also Stanford, MIT, Notre Dame, and other "top" universities that shine high up on the Best Colleges lists. For countless high schoolers (and even younger students), the parental, academic, and social pressures of "Where will you go to college?" are all too real, all too intimidating, and all too skewed against them.

For Harvard's most recent undergraduate crop -- the Class of 2026 -- 61,221 students applied, and a scant 1,984 were accepted. That's a 3.24 percent acceptance rate, which has flavors of The Hunger Games' motto, "May the odds be ever in your favor." On a macro level, the chances of surviving through to completion are about the same.

The majority of applicants have all the test scores, grades, and extracurriculars that would be expected of qualified applicants. By default, they likely fall in the middle of the bell curve distribution. With thousands of high-achieving teenagers sending their applications in, standing out in that crowded playing field takes a special sauce that goes well beyond GPAs, SATs, AP Tests, and clubs.

So, what should You, a hopeful candidate, do?

The Practical

Start early

I've worked with many students in their Junior year who are trying to figure out their story in a nutshell (or 650 words) for the first time. It can be done, and takes a lot of intensive soul searching for some young people to be able to present themselves confidently. I've also worked with other students who grew up believing all the accolades they've been told by their doting parents and may not recognize that they are not as objectively impressive as they've been led to believe. Again, through a lot of soul searching we've managed to calibrate them into interesting and likable candidates. The one asset that would make the process less painful to many applicants is starting earlier in the journey of self-discovery.

I recommend students and their parents be cognizant about the college application process when the students are freshmen or sophomores in high school. They should not be so hyper-focused as to try filling the applications out years in advance but it would be helpful for everyone to know what will eventually be expected of the student when application season arrives. Knowing well in advance the types of questions that are asked of applicants can help calibrate areas where a candidate should focus during their formative high school years. If you look at different applications, you'll notice many questions revolve around the candidate's interests, what gets them excited, what they are "passionate" about (a grossly overused word in applications). They don't focus on "tell me why your course selections are more difficult or distinguishing than other students" or "how did you make your GPA so high?" or "Tell us about all the late nights you worked." And that's a good thing, because applicants are being given the opportunity to be recognized for pursuing interests or goals that really matter to them. The problem is most students don't know they are allowed to go wild on exploring their interests because they're so focused on keeping up in class.

The best way I can explain to teenagers how they should think about the way they appear to the outside world, for the purposes of college applications (and then well beyond college) is to think about their "branding." For example, I'd describe Taylor Swift as a musician and songwriter who takes a stand and speaks out on issues she believes in. I ask my students to think about how they would like to be described, and we can work backwards from there on deciding what type of credentials and credibility could be acquired to be known as such.

Forget "passion"

One of the worst questions teens get interrogated on is "What are you passionate about?" When I was a teenager, I had no idea what I was passionate about, I just knew what I liked to do, what I was reasonably good at doing, what I liked to do but was pretty bad at doing, and what I did not like doing at all. If I was forced to say I was passionate about something, being an insecure teenager, I would probably lose all interest in whatever it was I chose for fear of being obligated to love it forever going forward.

Once, when I was speaking to high school students and their parents in China about U.S. colleges, a mother came up to me and said her daughter wanted to go to Wharton (incorrectly assuming I, from Wharton, had a superpower of getting students accepted as a favor to their parents). What stands out in my mind was the mother trying to impress me by saying, "My daughter is passionate about marketing!" I informed her that no 16-year-old is passionate about marketing. I knew her daughter wasn't, the daughter knew she wasn't, but the nuance was lost on her mother in her efforts to impress.

There have been some students who ask me if they should focus on either Interest A or Interest B, thinking that one of the choices would somehow be looked upon better by the faceless, amorphous application committees. My answer is usually, "I actually don't care which one you choose, just as long as you actually want to do it." Students (but more often their parents) fret that the student may pursue an interest and then (gasp!) eventually decide they don't like it and want to go in another direction, potentially "wasting" time and energy. I tell them that's perfectly fine and it's okay to change directions along the individual journey of self-discovery and personal development. It's just as important to know what you don't like as it is to know what you do like. If an interest or discipline is forced onto any student (or any adult for that matter), they'll likely make an effort to engage dutifully for a while and try to do it well. Once they realize they genuinely do not enjoy spending the time doing whatever it is, it would be both a shame and a crime for adults to force them to continue. I want my students to spend their time, especially their free time, doing something they truly enjoy (besides vaping) because that's when they will sincerely try to make themselves better at whatever they are interested in.

I like to have 1-on-1 interviews with my students to hear their stories and I'll often pull at threads of the conversation, asking a lot of "Tell me more about...." to dig deeper into what drives them. One of my students said he loved playing video games. Naturally his parents hated hated hated it, but he loved it. This gamer was able to articulate that he liked strategizing with his friends online and planning attacks. Sometimes their attacks worked, sometimes they didn't, and the failures were just as exciting as the victories. To him, it wasn't just rocket launchers and explosions. Video games were his version of chess, with rocket launchers and explosions. He was able to create an insightful essay about what gaming means to him, and he showed his craft in a light that was refreshing and probably insightful and intriguing to many reviewers.

Pull, don't push

Keep in mind, with single-digit acceptance rates, college admissions offices are forced to find more reasons to say No to an applicant than to say Yes. To put it bluntly (and I apologize sincerely for sounding insensitive here) they have to sort the chaff from the wheat, regardless of how valuable and unique and special each individual piece of chaff may be. It's a numbers game. Admissions officers have to cut over 90 percent of the applicants early in the review process so they can get to work selecting the final happy few.

There are two ways to approach applications (and relationships, jobs, and life in general for that matter). The first, and most common way high schoolers are trained from an early age is to try to meet or exceed the stated profile of what an "ideal" candidate might look like -- suitable GPA and test scores, school honors and awards (it seems most every resumé I've seen includes National Merit Scholar), leadership roles in school-sponsored clubs, team sports, and community service. [The fact that community service is mandatory in many schools seems to defeat the point.] Many (actually, most) high schoolers don't know any better than to do what they're told by their school counselors and peers. When it comes time to apply to college, these applicants are hindered by trying to promote their accomplishments, hard work, and efforts to the college reviewers, basically pleading "Pick me! Pick me!" and hoping they don't look like everyone else, but they mostly do look like most everyone else because they've walked the same paths as everyone else for the last three years.

The other way – Our Way – is to approach the application process by presenting yourself in such a distinctive light that colleges will say, "We've got to get this student to enroll here because if we don't, they'll certainly be accepted somewhere else." Of course, it's much preferred to have colleges clamoring over an applicant (provided You are that applicant) and creating options for yourself to choose from. It's a daunting prospect and one that young people typically aren't used to, but that is what's required to stand out among tens or hundreds of thousands of applicants.

Think about how the environmental advocate Greta Thunberg would write her application. She most certainly would not position herself as someone who met a school's stated requirements as her strength. Instead, I imagine she would write about global issues important to her, how she has developed subject matter knowledge on the issues, and how she is determined and committed to focusing on her mission into the future. She would state clearly if she'd like to attend the school in question. The admissions committee would likely recognize that a person like Greta Thunberg will continue to thrive, grow, and succeed, whether she goes to their school or not. What school wouldn't want an applicant with that level of boldness and conviction? Understandably, you likely will not be on a Time magazine cover too soon, but nevertheless you have the ability to develop subject matter knowledge in whatever area you choose and you can take that as far as you desire.

Emulate

It's intimidating to do something for the first time. First public speech. First performance. First ask. First interview. First groundbreaking discovery. Fortunately, it's all been done by someone or many others before you. Those predecessors may or may not be of high school age, and there's no reason to limit your aspirations to your current age group. It's understandable that high schoolers might not have any idea whatsoever how to go from where they are currently to where they aspire to be, in any area. Comfort yourself by recognizing there are many adults in the same boat. I tell my students to think about people they admire in their field, the really big people in their field, not merely the best high schooler in their field. Why does that person impress them? What did they do? How did they do it? What did their journey look like and, breaking it down into baby steps, what things did they do to make progress on themselves? Are there any aspects of what they did that we could follow, mimic, copy, or improve upon? Baby steps are fine in this regard. What elements can we emulate from a successful person's journey so we are not forced to reinvent the wheel?

When I've broken accomplishments down in this manner, it becomes dramatically easier for some of my students to view the imposing mountain in front of them as shorter, more digestible walks that might realistically be achievable to some degree. Put one foot in front of the other, and it's okay to walk where someone else marked the trail.

Understand the process

When I was an admissions reader, it was a seasonal position that paid a small hourly stipend. I didn't do it for the money. I did it because I wanted to stay involved with my school as an alumnus and I could work in my slippers at home. As a reader, my role was to review applications and provide initial summary and feedback on what I was seeing. As applications got winnowed down through rounds of review, the admissions reviewers would continue paring down the pile of candidates until the few were chosen. I worked in the early stages of the review process. During any admissions season I would review anywhere from 70 to 125 applications, depending on my availability.

The Admissions Office administration I worked for directed us readers to spend no more than 25 minutes per application, so that we could process two applications per hour. With 25 minutes to review an entire digital folder, that meant I had about 15 minutes to read everything -- transcripts, essays, resumé, at least two letters of recommendation -- and about 10 minutes to write about 1 page of commentary on what I saw. Importantly, one question I had to answer for each application was, "Would this candidate be a good addition to the school community?"

With 15 minutes to assess a candidate's qualities, I tended to not spend more than a minute on school transcripts and test scores, mostly because they were roughly all the same. If someone got a perfect GMAT score I'd notice it, but otherwise the vast, vast majority of applicants all fell within the acceptable range of grades and scores. Grades and test scores were undistinguishing when every single person was a high achiever.

There was only one case out of all the applications I reviewed where I ended up writing "I do not believe this candidate can handle the workload of the degree program" because they really did not have the academic or work experience needed. But bless them for trying.

Bear in mind that 25 minutes to do all the reading and then writing is not a lot of time, and reading six applications would take a frenetic three hours. After reading eight applications my brain would be headed toward mush, if not already there, as the review work required a combination of speed reading, rapid assessment, searching for distinctive highlights, and speed writing. This is important for you to understand because many applicants default to thinking about themselves when they write their essays. It's natural to do so. They're being asked to talk about themselves after all. Instead, applicants should write thinking about the perspective of the tired, overworked, bleary-eyed reader. You want to make the process as easy and convenient to the review board. We'll discuss specific ways to achieve that in this book.

What matters most in an application?

The vast majority of applicants I reviewed fell within a respectable range of competency with grades and scores, so that data did not tell me enough about any single person to distinguish them. To try and gauge a candidate's strength of application the three areas I focused on were, in order: their essays, their resumé, and then their recommendations.

Essays

Again -- and this is important -- I wasn't getting paid particularly well so reviewing applications was more a labor of like (it wasn't love) with an aftertaste of me doing charity work for a multi-billion-dollar university endowment. There were two types of essays that resonated with me while all the rest got blurred into the background. The first type of essay that stood out was one where the writer was discussing something important to them, which might have been a personal or professional issue, and the writer ended up educating me on some topic or issue so I felt as though I exited their essays incrementally smarter than when I entered. With those essays I gained knowledge points in lieu of a better hourly rate. The second type of essay was one where it was written in such a way as to be a meaningfully enjoyable read. The prose or narrative was done so well that reading didn't feel like work. A small, small handful were even laugh out loud clever. The best essays were the ones that I could remember the next day and recall fondly. Applicants who could accomplish either of these types of essays received high marks from my reviews.

The essays that I grew numb reading were those where the applicant stated how smart, unique, or charismatic they believed themselves to be without providing compelling, credible evidence to back it up. There is a major difference between merely telling a reader about how you, the hopeful applicant, might be a fastidious learner or a natural leader or an empathetic human being versus showing those characteristics through believable, meaningful examples of you doing so. "Show, don't tell," is an important standard to maintain throughout your application process (including in your eventual interviews) that we will work on together throughout this process.

In our present world of AI, every essay is going to be written well, some will be flawless. The landscape has changed and now everyone can be articulate, insightful, reflective or whatever else one chooses to prompt ChatGPT or other AI to craft. Put frankly, essays don't matter nearly as much as they used to, but evidence does. Being able to credibly demonstrate that you've somehow made a ripple, an impact, or a difference is what will set your application apart from the others. Also, the more one has "accomplished" (whatever that means, as it can be different for every person), the easier it becomes to write an application essay in plain English, more matter-of-factly stating what you've done, are doing, and intend to do going forwards. When an applicant does not have a lot to show, that's harder to do and they may end up pontificating philosophically about "stuff," which may be more generic or forgettable to the reviewers. It's not necessarily fair, it just is. More on that later.

Resumés

Reading student resumés is usually pretty painful. Mostly because the writers don't recognize that the readers at competitive schools are jaded adults who are not particularly impressed with moderate accomplishments that are presented in an inflated manner especially when so many others have the same credentials. Don't get me wrong, it IS a worthy accomplishment to be inducted into the

National Honor Society or any of the many other academic societies out there but reviewers are a tough crowd. If it's an award issued to high schoolers anywhere in the world, it's safe to assume previous members of every academic, sport, or extra-curricular society have already described what it is in depth, so the reviewers get it. [Goodness knows, I wasn't a National Honor Society member during my high school nor were my grades notable so I applaud all those who did accomplish it and are seeking to distinguish even further in this book.]

A well-written resumé, on the other hand, can demonstrate a student is deeply familiar with their activities and understands which parts are most meaningful and productive on a larger scale. It's also an opportunity to show what the student has accomplished, rather than being just a passive club member who sits in the room once a week. Speaking of which...

Not Student Clubs

Every high school club seems to have a President, Vice President, or other exalted titles for students to fill and it's often unclear what any of that means, if they mean anything at all. Where possible, it's important for candidates to show they were actively involved in some way beyond chairing the meetings or doing a fundraiser. One club many of my students list (initially) that comes across as non-meat filler is the Eco Club, where it is commonly described as students getting together and discussing the environment once a week. It's hard to gauge if there's any actual action or output that's generated by this club besides a modest fundraiser so I recommend either doing something big or not listing it as an activity. Putting posters around school and talking at assembly for Earth Day? Nice but not extraordinary. Cleaning up 10,000 pounds of trash from your local community park or abandoned urban lot? Pretty Impressive. It's better to have a few solid activities rather than a laundry list of low-impact schedule occupiers.

Recommendations

When I was a teenager, I was a student at the Bronx High School of Science, one of New York City's specialized public schools where I had to take a standardized test to place into the school. Bronx Science was one of three science-focused high schools in New York City: Stuyvesant, Bronx Science, and Brooklyn Tech. Stuyvesant in Manhattan required the highest score, Bronx Science was second highest, and Brooklyn Tech was third. Every day I commuted from Queens to Manhattan to the Bronx by subway, which took 1 hour and 10 minutes each way. Our school was noted for its high number of Westinghouse Science Talent Search competition winners (which became the Intel competition and now the Regeneron competition). There were a lot of smart people in my year, much smarter and more disciplined than I was. One student in my class, John, discovered a new bacteria and named it the John bacteria. Even our bullies were smart. One guy was expelled for spraying freon on another student – noogies and pink bellies were too pedestrian apparently. I gravitated to the mechanical engineering side and spent my extra time drawing components and machines using T-squares and triangles to my heart's content, even winning some drafting competitions as my "thing."

When I was applying to colleges, I didn't know my counselor until my Junior-year fall term, and she knew nothing about me (nor did she seem interested in learning anything about me either). And I don't blame her. I wasn't particularly remarkable; I didn't get to name a bacteria after myself or anything like that. I was adept with mechanical pencils and making really nice, accurate drawings in my engineering and architecture classes. I'm sure I got a glowing recommendation from my mechanical drawing mentor, but that's about it.

The best advice I can give, not just for college applications but for the long-term is for students to develop a handful of mentor relationships in the first year or two of high school with their most inspiring teachers, advisors, or coaches. I would have benefited greatly had I done so, having someone who could guide me with their maturity and wider perspective. But I didn't even know I could ask. Some relationships will blossom naturally; however, it is perfectly acceptable to ask a teacher, "Would it be okay if I come to you from time to time to help me figure out how to navigate classes and school?" or something along those lines. Some may say they're too busy, but others will not. Having a rejection should not be discouraging because it will help redirect your energies to mentors more inclined to take an interest in your success.

Standout recommendations are those where the teacher or coach is articulate and an enthusiastic proponent wanting to see the candidate succeed in college. The ideal recommender can also envision the student succeeding far beyond college, appreciating that the student's courage, intellect, and compassion will empower them to achieve meaningful and impactful future accomplishments. In high school and throughout your larger life, give thought to identifying and developing your support network. Bear in mind that your mentors should not only be those people who will applaud everything you do or gently shepherd you along the way. Some of my most valuable mentors have been people who have told me – sometimes harshly but always with my best interests in mind – to stop screwing around and get back to work. And they were right at the time when they were giving me hard truths I needed to hear.

Chapter 2 – The Tao of Applications

Before I begin working with any of my students, I make it a point to tell them and their parents that what I want to accomplish with them is not to focus on getting into one particular school but rather, once acceptance offers are made, for them to have received as many acceptances as possible to choose from. I want to help create options for my students so they can choose where to go. I've said the same thing to my own children. I do recognize and appreciate the brand value that a top college name can bring to a future resumé, but at the end of the day I want my children to be happy, engaged, and inspired wherever they choose to go. There's absolutely no point in a young person going to, say, Yale, if they end up being miserable. I'd much rather see them go somewhere where they will thrive for the long haul, regardless of the school's name.

In a few instances, I have had to turn down working with overbearing parents who are laser-focused on getting their child into a specific college while not sufficiently considering their child's wishes and aspirations.

In a different situation, there was one student I had who, eventually, admitted that he did not want to go to college, and if he did go it might be to his local community college. I wasn't particularly surprised at hearing this as it became obvious over time that his heart and head were somewhere else when we worked together. My best advice to him was that he needed to sit down with his parents and repeat to them what he shared with me, and have an adult conversation about it. He and I parted on good terms because I listened to what he wanted to say, rather than try to push him where others expected him to go.

It's important for high school students to understand that they can thrive and even surpass their wildest expectations wherever they ultimately choose to go to college, provided they are willing to engage and apply themselves in whatever it is they choose to pursue. The name on their school should not define them. Instead, they should look to be a prime example of what's best about the school they end up attending.

Intrinsic versus extrinsic values

Intrinsic values are ideals such as "I want to be challenged and excited about the work I do," and "I want to make an impact," and "I want to be present with the people I care about." Extrinsic values might include, "I want to be valedictorian," or "I want to be a millionaire," or "I want to be famous," or "I want to be a partner at a private equity firm." I tell my students to figure out what they value and prioritize their intrinsic values above everything else.

The best and most creative techies, artists, researchers, and other subject matter experts are the ones who do what they do because it provides them inner joy and satisfaction. These individuals usually have the intrinsic values of wanting to be continually challenged, engaged, fascinated, and inspired by what they are doing and also have some modicum of fun while doing so. When life kicks down a person who focuses on intrinsic values, they still know who they are and can eventually overcome their adversities.

A person with extrinsic values might equate their self-worth to their net worth, which is not a good place to be. When a person who focuses on extrinsic values gets body slammed by life, such as a "failure", a market crash, infamy or other unfortunate event, those individuals can lose sight of who they are because what they valued has been taken away. If their net worth, GPA, job title, or other social capital disappears, so might an extrinsically focused person's sense of self, which is never healthy.

There's a saying (attributed to many different authors so nobody knows who started it, but it's insightful nevertheless), "Comparison is the thief of joy." Extrinsic values are often someone else's life we want. Social media often showcases the best moments of people's lives: their wins, expensive stuff, vacations, and perfectly staged photos. It rarely shows their struggles, setbacks, or insecurities. Comparing your everyday reality to someone else's curated content can lead to feelings of inadequacy and pressure to perform. Remember: everyone's life has highs and lows, even if they don't show it.

It's only four years

College is great and a huge milestone, but in the span of one's life it's only a stepping stone toward all that follows. I realize that may be a small comfort for a student to hear while they are in the throes of the application process yet is still important to recognize and appreciate. High schoolers have decades more of frustration ahead of them so you should remember that college is one phase of many to come.

The Worst Advice for High School Students I Have Ever Heard

College admissions bring a flood of advice, some helpful and some awful. The worst I've seen came from a consultant on Instagram [Note: not one of our consultants!] who encouraged high school students go to their school's auditorium when it was empty and stage a photo of themselves standing on the stage, pretending to speak to an audience (of course, the empty seats would not be visible, just the speaker, stage and backdrop, perhaps even with a podium for effect.) to give the illusion of being an inspiring public speaker.

The problem is not just that it looks fake. It is fake. It tells students to value image over substance, which undercuts everything that matters in the application process and beyond. The allure of such advice is easy to understand in today's image-obsessed culture. College admissions have become fiercely competitive, and students feel intense pressure to craft the perfect narrative. The idea of presenting oneself as a confident, in-demand leader who inspires audiences may seem like an attractive shortcut to stand out in a crowded applicant pool. After all, a picture is worth a thousand words, and in this case, it may seem to say, "I am a person of influence and ideas."

Authenticity is what admissions officers respect. They want real interests and real stories. A staged photo raises questions and risks the student's credibility. Even modest achievements that come from genuine effort carry far more weight. Staging an image to feign accomplishments is fundamentally dishonest. It's an attempt to shortcut the hard work and dedication required to become a genuine subject matter expert or an inspiring speaker. Worse still, it teaches students that appearances matter more than substance, which is a message that is deeply damaging to anyone's personal development.

Bad advice like that also weakens confidence. Students who fake accomplishment often feel like impostors. Those who do the work, no matter how small, build lasting pride and resilience. And there is the matter of ethics. Pretending to be what you're not sets a poor example. Integrity matters, not just for admissions but for life. Colleges seek individuals who will contribute honestly and meaningfully, not those who cut corners.

The better path is clear: pursue real interests, value small wins, and tell the truth about your experiences. That is what creates impact, not staged illusions.

Section 2 – Tactics, Techniques and Procedures

Table of Contents

Topic	Page
Chapter 3 – Tactics, Techniques, Procedures	17
Chapter 4 – Tactics	19
Know Thyself	19
Lead with Humility	20
Treat the Application Process Like a Job	20
Become Subject Matter Knowledgeable	21
Impersonate an Adult	22
Advocate for Yourself	24
Advocate for Others	24
Create Information and Generate Deliverables	25
Develop your Personal Brand	25
Learn How to Write Your Story	26
Practice Frequent Self-Care	26
Chapter 5 – Know thyself	29
Myers Brigg Type Indicator	30
Chapter 6 – Lead with Humility (i.e., Don't be an Ass)	33
Chapter 7 – Treat Your Application Process Like a Job	35
Show up on time	38
Use a CRM to manage your opportunities	38
Chapter 8 – Become Subject Matter Knowledgeable	41
Pay Attention	42
Curated news	43
Trickle-feed your learning	44
Turbocharge your learning	45
Certificates versus certifications	45
So what?	46
Learn what you need to get the job done	46
Membership Societies	47
Be wary of college enrichment courses	48
Workshops and hands-on learning	48

Chapter 9 – Impersonate an Adult 49
- Conferences, conventions, and industry events 49
- Learn from industry practitioners about their craft 51
  - Open mic nights 51
  - Public events 52

Chapter 10 – Advocate for Yourself 53
- Broaden your perspective 53
  - Learn how to pitch 53
  - Mr., Ms., Mrs., Mx. 54
  - Definitely gonna give you up 54
  - Learn how to write a cover letter 54
  - Nothing ventured, nothing gained 55
- Collect rejections 57
- Leave a mark 58
  - Order business cards, use them judiciously 59

Chapter 11 – Advocate for Others 61
- Directories of volunteer opportunities 61
  - VolunteerMatch 62
  - LinkedIn Volunteers 62
  - Amnesty International Decoders 62
  - Smithsonian Digital Volunteers 62
  - World Youth Alliance 63
- Carve your own Path 63
- Join a Board 63

Chapter 12 – Create Information and Generate Deliverables 65
- Public Speaking 66
- How to Apply to Give a TEDx Talk 67
  - Typical TEDx application questions 73
- How to get an Article Published 74
  - Sample Pitch Letter 76
- Our first and foremost rule for writing an Op-Ed or voicing your opinion publicly in any setting 79
  - Publishing Tips 80
  - Types of Media Outlets to Consider 81
    - National 81
    - Regional 81
    - Local outlets 81
    - Industry-focused 81
    - Community-focused 81
    - Third-party blogs 82
  - Open platforms for publishing 82
  - DIY Publishing 83

- Resources for better writing 83
- How to Publish a Book Fast 84
  - Production Tips 87
  - Marketing Tips 88
- How to Create an Online Course 90
- Submit your Research Paper to Conferences 93
  - Directories of industry conferences 94
    - CFP List 94
    - 200+ Best Conferences to Attend 95
    - WikiCFP 95
    - Conal Conference Alerts 95
- How to Exhibit your Art 96
  - Exhibition Channels 96
    - Self-curated shows and pop-up exhibits 96
    - Non-curated group shows 97
    - Publications or online galleries 97
    - Curated group shows 98
    - Curated member-only shows 98
    - Gallery exhibits 98
    - Museum exhibits 98
  - Directories of Open Call Opportunities 99
    - Art Call 99
    - Art Connect 100
    - Call For Entry 100
  - Learn about the Business of Art 100
    - Praxis Center for Aesthetic Studies 100
- How to get Quoted in the Media 101
  - Helpareporter.com 101
  - Qwoted.com 103
- How to Create your Portfolio Website 104
  - Website Hosting 105
- How to Make your Deliverables Look, Sound, and Feel Better 106
  - Stock image resources 106
    - Unsplash.com 106
    - Pexels.com 106
    - Pixabay.com 106
    - Adobe Stock 106
  - Custom illustrations 107
  - Desktop publishing 107
    - Adobe InDesign 107
  - Printing resources 107
    - Docucopies.com 107
    - PrintNinja.com 107

Chapter 13 – Develop Your Personal Brand 109

- Understand how colleges stalk you ... 109
  - Student data for sale ... 109
  - College websites are watching your clicks ... 110
- Before you apply, clean your social media ... 111
  - At a minimum, set all accounts to Private ... 112
    - Facebook privacy settings ... 113
    - Instagram privacy settings ... 113
    - Snapchat privacy settings ... 113
    - TikTok privacy settings ... 113
    - Twitter privacy settings ... 114
  - Even better, create a 2nd account and don't cross-fertilize ... 114
  - Don't use Google, Facebook or automatic logins for other sites ... 114

Chapter 14 – Learn how to Tell Your Story ... 117
- AI is completely rewriting the Ivy League college admissions game. ... 117
- Our Manual of Style ... 118
  - Avoid and eschew unnecessarily descriptive scene-setting embellishment and overly-lengthy extended word-consuming verbosity ... 118
  - Topics to avoid* ... 119
  - Words and phrases to avoid ... 119
  - Wordplay ... 120
- Writing habits to develop ... 120
  - Do the *New York Times* crossword puzzle regularly ... 120
  - Audiobooks ... 121

Chapter 15 – Practice Frequent Self-Care ... 123
- Mental Health is the cornerstone of well-being ... 123
  - Find Your Calm ... 123
  - Unplug yourself ... 124
  - Practice Effective Time Management ... 124
  - Prioritize Quality Sleep ... 125
  - Release Endorphins, Reduce Stress ... 125
  - Lean on Your Support System: You Are Not Alone ... 125
  - Seek Support: Reach Out When Needed ... 126
  - Strengthen your self-awareness ... 126
  - Understand self-regulation ... 126
  - Embrace a Growth Mindset ... 127

Chapter 3 – Tactics, Techniques, Procedures

Let's get down to business. If we're going to conquer the world, let's do so in a methodical, actionable manner using an array of powerful Tactics, Techniques, and Procedures.

Tactics are high-level aspirations, techniques are specific strategies you can take to accomplish those tactics, and procedures are the step-by-step actions required to perform the techniques. For example, in Star Wars – A New Hope:

Tactic: We should stop the Galactic Empire from terrorizing us with their Death Star.

Technique: A carefully placed photon torpedo can blow up their Death Star.

Procedure: Step-by-step instructions on how to shoot photon torpedoes at this hole they left open on the Death Star...

I've identified the following 11 tactics that you can pursue to distinguish yourself dramatically from the competition when it comes to you applying to college. Importantly, some or all of these tactics can be valuable well beyond college for your career, your relationships, and for the rest of your life.

1. **Know Thyself** – Learn how to evaluate objectively your strengths, weaknesses, motivations, and aspirations.
2. **Lead with Humility** – Learn how to present your capabilities in a credible and authentic manner.
3. **Treat the Application Process Like a Job** – Learn how to manage the daunting application process with the least pain possible.
4. **Become Subject Matter Knowledgeable** – Learn how to refine your skills and deepen your expertise.
5. **Impersonate an Adult** – Learn how to deftly navigate the big, wide world.
6. **Advocate for Yourself** – Learn how to advocate for yourself like an adult.
7. **Advocate for Others** – Learn how to advocate for others and turn your compassion into action.
8. **Create Information and Generate Deliverables** – Learn how to add constructively to the conversation around your interests.

9. **Develop Your Personal Brand** – Learn how to curate your personal brand.//
10. **Learn How to Write Your Story** – Learn how to write.
11. **Practice Frequent Self-Care** – Learn how to protect and nurture your mental and emotional well-being throughout your journey.

In this section we will discuss the impact of each tactic to give you a 360-degree view of how cumulatively these tactics can help you become absurdly unique, ridiculously talented, and brilliantly promising. Then we go into a wide range of techniques you can employ along with step-by-step instructions.

Chapter 4 – Tactics

The collective goal of these tactics is to provide you with the tools, skills, and knowledge to make smart, informed decisions that can help you reach as high as you aspire.

Accomplishments should be cumulative. You don't ever want to grow up to be the person who peaked in high school – the sad adults who still recount their varsity football days or prom queen glory as their greatest accomplishment. Instead, every time you make meaningful progress or achieve a small victory, you should build upon that milestone to advance toward your bigger goals. If you are committed to your on-going personal growth, when you find yourself reaching a goal, chances are you'll already have a larger follow-on goal in mind that's waiting to challenge your ever-growing capabilities.

Here is why the 11 Tactics matter:

Know Thyself

"So tell me about yourself" is one of the hardest questions to answer for most high schoolers in an interesting, distinctive way. When I ask new clients this question, nearly everyone starts off by saying:

"I'm a junior at…."

Zzzzzzzzzzzzzz

Those types of responses are factually accurate but entirely forgettable, especially when other applicants are queued up to tell their stories right after you. Don't be discouraged; however, because I'll grant that bombing on this question is not necessarily your fault. Or at least it's avoidable if you want to make it so. (You might be surprised to realize that it's often hard for many adults to answer this question in any sort of interesting manner, such as in job interviews.]

I've observed that a person may have a hard time describing themselves because they don't actually know who they are. Layer on the burden of being a teenager and it can be even more baffling. To be able to talk about yourself, and not merely run through your resumé, I strongly recommend taking objective, third-party assessments of your personality to see how others would see you and describe you. Fortunately, through some quality online assessments that are available, you can do this inexpensively and receive extensive commentary on what, objectively measured, makes you tick.

I'm partial to the Myers-Brigg assessment but there are lots of others out there. Feedback I've received from people who have taken these tests is that the assessments are highly accurate identifying a person's strengths. Importantly, they also identify the things a person does not enjoy or is not best suited for. [I'm avoiding using the term "weaknesses" here because it's important to understand not everyone can be or do everything. Everyone is better at some things and not as interested in others.] From a conversation standpoint, being able to share what you don't like is as revealing as what you do enjoy and can also demonstrate self-awareness and maturity, which can be used to your benefit during the application and interview process.

Lead with Humility

A whole lot of high schoolers live in a bubble where they receive continual praise for nearly everything they do. And that's fine, people should be supportive in general. A messy wrinkle may arise when the recipient of constant praise starts to believe it. There's nothing less believable than when an applicant writes in their essays how smart they are.

Margaret Thatcher, the UK Prime Minister explained it best when she said, "Being powerful is like being a lady. If you have to tell people you are, you aren't."

Similarly, if you have to tell people you're smart, well… You figure it out.

Over the span of my life, I've had the unpleasant realization that people are usually the exact opposite of how they outwardly describe themselves. "I'm a nice guy." "I don't hold grudges." "I'm really smart."

There's incredible value in showing humility in yourself and having enough confidence to allow your work to speak for itself. Not only will admissions officers notice the difference, so will many others that you'll encounter throughout your life. Show, don't tell. If you've put the genuine effort into creating something, writing something, inventing something, performing something to the best of your current abilities, then let your work speak for itself, without needing you to tell people why you think it's good. Whatever opinions people form on their own will be more valuable and convincing than anything you can try to convince them of about your talents.

Treat the Application Process Like a Job

One person I worked with was applying to 17 top schools across the U.S., and was qualified for each of them. In alphabetical order they included:

Brown, CalTech, Carnegie Mellon, Columbia, Cornell, Dartmouth, Harvard, Harvey Mudd, MIT, Princeton, Rensselaer Polytechnic, Stanford, UPenn, Georgia Tech, UCSD, UC Berkeley, and Vanderbilt.

Across those applications:

14 started with the Common App essay;

> 57 supplemental essays were required;
>
> 8 allowed for a portfolio submission; and
>
> 1 required a video submission (Brown).

Fifth-seven well-written, compelling, and memorable supplemental essays is too much work for any human being, let alone a high school student with homework and a social life. Treating their application process like a job, we created a matrix identifying the specific theme each essay was asking (for example, "What passion, inspiration, or experience led to your area of study?"). We identified 13 major themes, and then sorted the 57 essays into their respective themes. We made note of the different word maximums for each essay, then noted in each theme which school allowed for the longest essay. In the theme, we would work on the longest essay first, making it as strong as possible, telling the best story we could with the most details. From there we could cut the longest essays down and reduce word count to meet each applications' requirements, which is much easier than starting with a short essay and expanding on it to meet bigger word counts. In several cases we were able to reduce, reuse, and recycle.

It was still a significant amount of work to accomplish, but we went from a near-impossible task to a manageable, intensive effort that resulted in a positive, happy outcome for the student.

Similarly with the portfolio submission, we started with the most demanding portfolio submission requirements, made the best portfolio possible, and then pared down for other applications.

The Brown video submission turned out to be stressful but still enjoyable to work on as the student crafted a thoughtful, complex deliverable that spoke to the level of quality output they were able to create.

Become Subject Matter Knowledgeable

You should know something about everything and everything about something.

It doesn't matter what exactly your "everything about something" subject is, as long as it's something you actually want to know, do, or understand more and more about each day. You're also not limited to only one deep subject, and you are allowed to change what's on that short list over time. For your own growth, your own ability to be interesting as a person, and -- let's face it -- your own ability to distinguish yourself among college applicants, you MUST invest the time, energy, and effort into yourself to know enough about something that people you respect in turn respect you for your particular set of skills.

The best thing about deep knowledge is that it can be about anything you genuinely care about. One of the best essays I once read in an application was from a woman who worked a corporate desk job by day and at night was lead singer in a punk rock band. Her essay on overcoming adversity was about how, after years of failing, she finally learned how to sing in the guttural, throaty, growling voice that was fundamentally important to an authentic punk rock sound. I learned so much unexpected perspective from her 500 words, and she included a YouTube link of one of her performances to show what she was capable of.

In another instance, I once spent time with a man who proudly and enthusiastically walked me through his Lego collection of architectural buildings and machines he built, which were prominently displayed in his living room. At first, I didn't understand why it was meaningful but he showed me Lego construction in an entirely new light – the way he saw it – which in turn increased my appreciation of something I hadn't previously given much thought to and also taught me to not be so quickly judgmental.

Also, the more you learn the more you earn. Not necessarily in dollars, but there have got to be boundless benefits to be reaped from the effort of making yourself better informed.

As a rule, whether in high school, college, or afterwards, it's a healthy habit to always be learning either in an academic or professional setting, online, or some other educational program. Always strive to hone your crafts and broaden your skills. Show that you are committed to deepening your subject matter knowledge. While you are still in high school, I highly recommend you look at online courses through Coursera, EdX, Udemy, LinkedIn Learning, or any of the many other sites that offer whatever you may be interested in. Obtaining certificates of completion when available is an added benefit to demonstrate you took the course seriously and to completion. On your resumé, it speaks well to show that you've put the time and effort into learning over and above your standard school curriculum.

Impersonate an Adult

We all live in our own bubble. Some people's bubbles are larger than others. Make yours as large and as interesting as possible.

Many high schoolers are perfectly happy to operate within the comfortable boundaries of a bubble that primarily encompasses their high school ecosystem, organized activities, sports, and other "typical" teenager activities. Many of these activities are intended for teenagers to participate in, within a relatively safe and controlled environment. For many teenagers, that type of bubble might represent roughly 70 to 90 percent of their existence and interests. To stand out as an admissions candidate, that comfortable yet limited bubble should represent, say, 30 to 50 percent of your existence.

[Pause for screaming]

These are estimates. My estimates. And today I'm not the one who has to do the work of leaving that bubble, so you can determine how much you will or won't budge. Whatever you decide is fine with me, as long as you are fine with it. Stepping beyond high school, while still in high school, is more art than science. To do so requires you to be brave, bold, even bright (more on all of this later too).

As an example, not everybody is going to be Greta Thunberg, the environmental activist; however, she is a great example of a person who stepped well outside of a comfortable teenager bubble to explore the wide world around her. And to stir up some constructive mischief in the process to advocate for her cause.

One of the biggest obstacles I've observed that prevents high schoolers from venturing into the adult world is simply they haven't been told they are allowed to do so. Most high schoolers are programmed to ask for permission from authorities to be allowed to do things they desire to do. Parents, teachers, coaches, whomever. And I've found most adult authorities to be either woefully unimaginative, too busy to get involved, too trepidatious to let the young person take risks, or some combination of all these. And that's fine in most circumstances. There is a Japanese proverb that goes "The nail that sticks up gets hammered down." To stand out in the ocean of college applications; however, a candidate has to be the one nail sticking up.

If, for example, a motivated student expresses interest in computer science, their guidance counsellor might typically suggest they join their school's computer science club so they can add it to their extracurriculars list (the path of least resistance). Instead, that student should be encouraged to explore the BlackHat, RSA or DefCon conferences or go through the vastly educational process of successfully publishing an app on the App Store or Google Play. Aspiring artist? Pitch for exhibits at ArtConnect or group shows at real venues. The opportunities are boundless for anyone willing to look, in whatever their area of interest is. Importantly, every small milestone is a stepping stone for the next, bigger goal. My advice: Be Bold.

It's uncomfortable, even intimidating, for any student to step out of their high school bubble, which presents opportunity for those candidates seeking outsized mountains to summit. The most important requirement is that a person has genuine curiosity. I've worked with students who were also punk rock singers, Fortnite strategists, CRISPR researchers, and graffiti artists (correction: urban muralists) are were dedicated, inquisitive, and just plain fun to work. When I have the benefit of working early in the process with a Freshman, Sophomore, or Junior, our goal is to help them build genuine subject matter knowledge, which naturally makes them ever more inspired to dive deeper into their topic of choice. Outsized "grown up" accomplishments will arise throughout the journey.

My best advice to aspiring applicants: Don't do as you say, do as you do. Don't be afraid to slip or fail in pursuit of your goals because adults do it all the time. You don't have to start from scratch, either. There are countless people who have carved paths ahead of you that you can follow, learn from and emulate.

Granted, if the student still needs Mom or Dad to drive them, asking some permission is warranted and considerate of other people's time.

Advocate for Yourself

Learning how to advocate for yourself in the "adult" world is different than learning how to ask for permission. I view self-advocacy as seeking collaboration, partnership, information sharing, or other manner of exploration to advance a cause. Talk is easy, action takes work. To get what you want regarding your larger aspirations, you will have to become your own strongest advocate and break through that sometimes real, sometimes imaginary barrier that separates you from the larger world.

Asking permission is "Would it be okay if I go to your exclusive event..." whereas advocating would be more along the lines of "I would like to support your important work at your event by..."

Being able and willing to ask for help or guidance, pitching your ideas, presenting your credentials, being taken seriously, gaining access to suitable events, even writing a compelling cover letter are all important skills that can be learned, and are explained in the Techniques and Procedures chapters.

Advocate for Others

There's nothing less imaginative in an application than listing the mandatory community service you are required to do with everyone else in your grade. If your school forces you to be benevolent and caring, if only for 2 hours, and that's the only example of you being giving of yourself, that says a lot – or is it a little? – about you and your willingness to engage in issues bigger than yourself. (Yes, I'm being cynical when I say this, but mandatory community service is a common weakness I find in many of my client's draft applications.)

I do not recommend getting involved in charitable or activist causes just to have a line item on your resumé, that would be insincere and not the best use of your time. Provided you actually would like to get involved in advocacy or volunteer opportunities that may have lasting impact, there are endless opportunities you can explore. Many of the recommendations we will discuss to support major organizations can even be done remotely. It's well known that volunteering for causes meaningful to you is beneficial to your physical and mental health, provides a sense of purpose and teaches meaningful skills, and increases social interaction and nurtures existing and new relationships.[1]

If you have enough time before your applications are due so that you can show you've made a meaningful contribution and impact to a cause, by all means share it in your application. If you don't have enough time to impact your applications but still want to volunteer your time, energy, and resources, by all means do so. Hopefully you will still find the experience meaningfully satisfying and personally rewarding.

---

[1] "3 Health Benefits of Volunteering," Mayo Clinic Health System, n.d., https://www.mayoclinichealthsystem.org/hometown-health/speaking-of-health/3-health-benefits-of-volunteering.

Create Information and Generate Deliverables

There are countless types of deliverables you can create, such as songs, videos, art, or information that explains something to someone. The difference between a deliverable and an idea is that the deliverable can be shown, shared, and showcased. An idea just swirls around in your head and you have to explain what you want to do versus what you've done. Provided the quality of your work is solid, links to your deliverables can (and should) be included in resumés or applications to show that it and you are real.

Getting seen, heard, read, or otherwise published in any media (writing, music, art, research, or other area that interests you) requires a strong level of discipline to send out pitches, wait patiently, get rejected, refine your work if appropriate, and then repeat the process of sending out more pitches. It's not always easy, and that's why getting published or obtaining a platform to share your information can be a valuable credential.

I've helped students give TEDx Talks, have their articles and Op-Eds published, publish books, publish research, create online courses, exhibit in galleries and museums, create serious art portfolios, and other notable accomplishments that bolster their credibility as individuals who clearly are subject matter knowledgeable in their areas of interest. Getting published also demonstrates that independent third parties (such as editors, curators, peer reviewers) recognize the work as being worthy and valid.

As a writer, I'm partial to the incredible benefits publishing quality articles, essays, research, or other information can have on a person's resumé. Talk is cheap, everyone does it, but it is another thing entirely if you can point to a quality piece of work you've written. When I encourage many of my students to consider writing an article, the response I often hear is "Why would anyone care about what I have to say?" I view my students in the exact opposite light. "Why wouldn't people want to hear what you have to say?"

Young people have a perspective that is often unheard. I have found there is a readily-available audience interested in learning about our world and current events from a young person's thoughtful viewpoint.

Develop your Personal Brand

In our hyper-connected world, where the line separating our private lives and public-facing lives continues to thin, it's more important than ever for serious applicants to curate their outward-facing image while shielding their private lives from the general public. Developing a personal brand also forces you to decide what, in essence, is your essence. What do you want people to recognize you as or associate you with? What do you want to lead with?

Think like a movie star who has a good public relations team. They are careful to post online only those photos, videos, and messages that present them in some admirable light. All the mundane, sloppy, unfiltered personal information is kept hidden to protect their privacy, mental health, and safety.

Be fully aware that college admissions teams scan applicants' social media and online profiles. It can make or break a decision. Given that admissions teams are looking for reasons to say "No" more than "Yes," realize that your social media posts from Friday night parties are not as witty or clever as you think they are, at least not to overworked admissions officers. We'll discuss specific steps to wipe out any potentially negative information in your social media as well as promote more appealing content to craft your public persona.

Learn How to Write Your Story

Okay, this one is hard, I'll admit it. High schoolers are mostly taught how to write book reports, which don't necessarily need to be interesting, just written according to a points-based rubric (which makes words on the page even less engaging).

Ernest Hemingway was a writer who didn't waste words. He didn't use unnecessarily large words to try to sound impressive. He got to the point without noise or flowery narration.

When your application essays are strictly limited to 250, 500, or 650 words (or somewhere in between) every word counts. Before you can write like Hemingway, I strongly recommend you read Hemingway. Read and pay attention to different writing styles in general. Re-read *The Sun Also Rises* even if you already covered it in English, and remind yourself what concise, descriptive writing looks like. John Steinbeck is another concise yet powerful storyteller. *Cannery Row* is excellent when it comes to telling a memorable story concisely. He would have crushed his college essays.

Hemingway also is noted for advising "Write drunk, edit sober." I realize you, a high school student, have no concept what alcohol is, but what he meant was when you write, just get it all out of your mind in whatever form it comes out. It's fine to initially let your big, sloppy river of thoughts and ideas splash onto the page. Later, when you are in a clearer state of mind, go back and figure out how to resonate with your reader.

Practice Frequent Self-Care

Let's be honest, the college application process sucks. It blows. It's artificial pressure on you to keep up with the fast-moving pack of hundreds of thousands of people your age to move on to the next major stage of your life.

I said previously that I'll speak to you like an adult, so do understand that I don't want you to devote yourself to the strategies in this book at the expense of your genuine well-being. I am perfectly happy to push you to do things that are well outside your comfort zone, intimidating, and even exhausting, but only within the boundaries of your best judgment. Just as in all aspects of life, know when to say "When."

Self-care is the opposite of self-harm, and it's important for you to determine which side you want for yourself. I'll be sharing information and recommendations for you to consider to care for what truly matters: You.

At the back of my mind, I'm haunted by the knowledge that suicide is one of the leading causes of death among teenagers. According to Statista, in 2021, around 23 percent of U.S. college and university students reported having had non-suicidal self-injurious behaviors in the past year, and two percent reported having attempted suicide.

A student's potential despair from going to a college or university that is not right for them is enough reason not to laser focus on getting into any singular university. Instead, I want people who use this book to create multiple options (i.e., multiple acceptance letters) to choose from.

Think of this book as telling you how to run a marathon. Can you run a marathon? Sure, if you try hard enough and want to do so. It will be a tedious, oftentimes stressful, and painful, yet an ultimately rewarding experience. And hopefully along the training process you'll make sure to find moments of appreciation, humor, and relief that are encouraging enough to lace up your shoes again the next day. If you don't want to run a proverbial marathon then, simply, don't. Even if everyone around you is running past you. No harm, no foul. Let other people head their own way, you get to decide where you want to go.

Chapter 5 – Know thyself

"Know Thyself" is an ancient Greek aphorism inscribed in the pronaos of the Temple of Apollo in Delphi.

[Quick SAT primer here: an "aphorism" is a tersely phrased statement of a truth or opinion. A "pronaos" is the inner area of the portico of a Greek or Roman temple, leading to the cella. A "portico" is a patio; and a "cella" is an inner chamber.]

Know Thyself is used, often overused, as a quick fix ranging from Socrates to countless self-help books. The problem with this simple direction is that there is often a disconnect between who we are and who we *think* we are. How we project ourselves to the outside world may differ wildly from the screaming voices in our heads, and I would posit that is human nature. For individual mental health and self-acceptance, understanding what makes each of us tick in our own special way is valuable to know. What makes any of us tick also likely evolves over time as we enter different stages of our lives. Why this matters to you today is because college applications ask in various ways for you to tell them what makes you tick.

Throughout my life's journey I have encountered countless individuals whose self-image of who they are has been the polar opposite of how they are in practice. "I'm a nice guy," "I don't hold grudges," "I'm easygoing," and "I'm not racist" come to mind. I've also met other people who grossly discount their proven, admirable traits such as empathy, generosity, patience, and intellectual curiosity. It's hard to self-assess oneself accurately because internally everything is relative, it's hard to naturally know what a baseline for our different characteristics might be in the bubble of our individual minds.

Fortunately, there are objective assessments that can provide insight into individual strengths and values, which can help quantify and qualify what makes each of us our own person. And those assessments can be meaningfully helpful in gaining understanding into the types of situations, environments, and even people who energize us and help us thrive. One assessment I'm partial to are the Myers-Brigg Type Indicator (MBTI). This assessment can be taken online with immediate feedback and are a solid starting point to answering the incredibly intimidating question of "Tell me about yourself."

One crucially important thing to recognize in these assessments in that no "type" of personality is better or worse than any other being measured. Each type of personality – just like each type of human being -- has particular strengths that can be leveraged as well as other areas that may not be as effective for an individual. Learning how to play to one's strengths while be cognizant of less influential parts can help equip each of us to be our better or best selves.

Myers Brigg Type Indicator

In practical terms, the MBTI personality inventory seeks objectively to identify and categorize our different behaviors, perceptions, and judgments, which might otherwise seem random and varied to us, since we're the ones living it. MBTI seeks to measure a person across four different areas:

1. What types of environments do you prefer to be in? Are you more **extroverted** or **introverted**?

2. Do you accept basic information (MBTI calls this **Sensing**) or do you tend to search for meaning or interpretation of information (this is called **Intuition**)?

3. Are you more of a **Thinking** person or a **Feeling** person? Thinking people seek logic and consistency, while Feeling people seek to understand the circumstances and the people involved.

4. Do you prefer to have situations concluded and decided (this is called **Judging**) or are you comfortable with keeping situations open to additional input and options (this is called **Perceiving**).

The categories are abbreviated as follows:

Extraversion (E) or Introversion (I)

Sensing (S) or Intuition (N)

Thinking (T) or Feeling (F)

Judging (J) or Perceiving (P)

Assessing the two options in these four categories results in 16 different personality types that a person might fall into. It's important to note that no one type is better or worse than any other, they are all just different, which helps make our world the interesting kaleidoscope it is.

There are a plethora of websites that offer the MBTI test either free or for a fee. One site offering a free test is www.16personalities.com and there are many others out there.

The value of the MBTI is it helps inform you what types of situations you are more likely to thrive in. For example, I once took the MBTI as part of a leadership workshop, I was listed as being Introverted. I was a bit skeptical since I often participated in outward-facing public events, networking opportunities, and public speaking as part of my professional life. My workshop instructor was able to discern that, although I am out at public events a lot, I am likely exhausted afterwards, which was 100 percent true. I had not recognized that aspect since I assumed that was to be expected after such events. But it's not the same for Extroverted folks, who might come away even more energized after meeting people and mingling in crowds. The valuable takeaway for me in that realization was that I allowed myself not to feel "bad" or even "insufficient" because I felt exhausted after social events. Instead, I now plan accordingly to give myself recharging time or self-care time after big events, guilt free. Similarly, I am able to view situations (and life in general) from a more-informed lens, understanding the other aspects of my personality. I use that self-awareness to have a better understanding of my feelings, opinions, and reactions to different situations, environments, and people and thereby be able to conduct myself appropriately.

Chapter 6 – Lead with Humility (i.e., Don't be an Ass)

> "There is nothing noble in being superior to some other man. The true nobility is in being superior to your previous self."
>
> — W. L. Sheldon, Lecturer of the Ethical Society of St. Louis, 1897

> "The more I learn, the more I realize how much I don't know."
>
> — Albert Einstein, hair model

According to Psychology Today, the Dunning-Kruger effect is a cognitive bias in which some people wrongly overestimate their knowledge or ability in a specific area. This tends to occur because a lack of self-awareness prevents them from accurately assessing their own skills.[2] The people who are smart in a subject tend to recognize what they don't know, whereas people who are unintelligent don't know what they don't know because they don't have the context or perspective to see where they fall in the grand scheme of things. Basically, smarter people tend to underestimate how much they know, whereas dumber people overestimate their capabilities.

Also bear in mind that every person is strong in some areas and weaker in others. Sometimes, an individual may mistake their capability in one area as being transferable into other areas, assuming their success in Area A should naturally extend to Area B. Imagine, for instance, someone who was reasonably successful in running, say, a startup electric car company and – just because they could afford it – having the hubris to think they were uniquely qualified to run a giant social media platform and decide what constitutes free speech. Could you imagine what a disaster that would be?

Or think about some of the politicians making decisions that impact countless lives – if you look hard enough, you may notice that some decision makers are making decisions and taking positions that have nothing to do with what's going on in the real world. Rather, they may be misinterpreting facts and reality to fit into their skewed worldview. Such an approach may not truly benefit the public, but often does help win elections and re-elections so their wheel keeps turning.

There's incredible value in showing humility in yourself and having enough confidence to allow your work to speak for itself. Not only will admissions officers

---

[2] Psychology Today, "Dunning-Kruger Effect," n.d., https://www.psychologytoday.com/us/basics/dunning-kruger-effect.

notice the difference, so will many others that you'll encounter throughout your life. Show, don't tell. If you've put the genuine effort into creating something, writing something, inventing something, performing something to the best of your current abilities, then let your work speak for itself, without needing you to tell people why you think it's good. Whatever opinions people form on their own will be more valuable and convincing than anything you can try to convince them of about your talents.

Leading with humility is easier said than done because, if you aren't already doing so naturally, that would suggest you've been programmed over your life to do the opposite and may not be cognizant of doing so. I'm not saying it's your fault. I am; however, pointing this nuance out to you now so that we can adjust our course heading to enter more nourishing waters. It's okay to be confident but don't be cocky. It's okay to be assertive but don't be arrogant. It's better to be persuasive than pushy.

To be appropriately humble, it helps to remember your audience in any given situation. For the purposes of your college applications, remember that you are not writing to your teachers or your friends or to the general public. You are writing to overworked admissions staff members who have the task of reviewing tens or hundreds of thousands of application packages every year. It's safe to assume those individuals have seen it all, read it all, and have heard it all. Their job is to say No many, many more times than it is to say Yes to candidates. Assume they are well-intentioned and want students to succeed but also somewhat jaded and slightly cynical, as their role requires, to winnow down so many thousands of candidates.

It's not your place to tell the essay reviewers that your work is amazing, innovative, top-notch, important or insightful. Do your best work and let them form their own opinion. You can state with conviction why you believe the issue is important, what problem you are genuinely trying to solve or imbalance you are trying to address, or why the work is necessary. You can describe the work that you did and the results that were achieved, but do so objectively for impactful narrative.

It helps to express gratitude for the opportunities you have been afforded rather than sounding like you're doing the recipient a kindness by participating. I've read too many variations on the humblebrag "It was a highly important project so I was selected to lead it given my past performance...." Ugh. Groan. There are countless other, more tactful, ways to demonstrate your capabilities. A better approach to discuss participation in a high profile project could be, "I was fortunate to be assigned to a project with the impactful goal of...."

There is a distinction between the accomplishments of any organization you might be associated with and your individual accomplishments. I've read many essays where a student might volunteer at a big-name charity and spend sentences about the millions of lives the group impacts, which has nothing to do with the applicant's contribution to the cause. I've seen the same with applicants discussing internships at global banks, engineering firms, and other companies. It's great to put your efforts in context (i.e., that you volunteered or worked at a leading, competitive organization) but don't overstate, overestimate, or over explain your contribution. Experienced reviewers will see right through credential puffery.

Chapter 7 – Treat Your Application Process Like a Job

I mentioned that one person I worked with was applying to 17 top schools across the U.S., and was qualified for each of them. In alphabetical order they included:

Brown, CalTech, Carnegie Mellon, Columbia, Cornell, Dartmouth, Harvard, Harvey Mudd, MIT, Princeton, Rensselaer Polytechnic, Stanford, UPenn, Georgia Tech, UCSD, UC Berkeley, and Vanderbilt.

Across those applications:

14 started with the Common App essay;

57 supplemental essays were required;

8 allowed for a portfolio submission; and

1 required a video submission (Brown).

Fifth-seven well-written, compelling, and memorable supplemental essays is too much work for any human being, let alone a high school student with homework, responsibilities, and a social life. Treating their application process like a job, we created a matrix identifying the specific theme each essay was asking (for example, "What passion, inspiration, or experience led to your area of study?"). We identified 13 major themes, and then sorted the 57 essays into their respective themes. We made note of the different word maximums for each essay, then noted in each theme which school allowed for the longest essay. In the theme, we would work on the longest essay first, making it as strong as possible, telling the best story we could with the most details. From there we could cut the longest essays down and reduce word count to meet each applications' requirements, which is much easier than starting with a short essay and expanding on it to meet bigger word counts. In several cases we were able to reduce, reuse, and recycle.

It was still a significant amount of work to accomplish, but we went from a near-impossible task to a manageable, intensive effort that resulted in a positive, happy outcome for the student.

Similarly with the portfolio submission, we started with the most demanding portfolio submission requirements, made the best portfolio possible, and then pared down for other applications.

The Brown video submission turned out to be stressful but still enjoyable to work on as the student crafted a thoughtful, complex deliverable that spoke to the level of quality output they were able to create.

The spreadsheet we created is shown below, and you can create a similar version for your target schools:

Subtotal		Brown	Cal Institute of Technology	Carnegie Mellon	Columbia U	Cornell U	Dartmouth College	Georgia Tech
16								
	Submitted	Y/N	Y/N	Y/N	Y/N	Y/N	Y/N	Y/N
13	Common Application	Yes	Yes	Yes	Yes	Yes	Yes	Yes
5	Resume					Resume	Resume	
7	Portfolio	Yes			Yes		Yes	
57	# of Supplemental Essays	0	4	3	7	3	2	2
6	What passion, inspiration, experience led to your area of study?			300 words (define major)	For Columbia Engineering specifically, 200 words			300 words
5	Why do you want our school?				200 words	For Cornell Engineering, 650 words	100 words	
3	Why this program?					What 3 words describe Cornell Engineering		
6	What are you passionate about, excites you? (In general)						1 of 5 choices, 300 words, music	
7	What contribution have you made to family, school, or community?				200 words			300 words
4	Introduce / describe yourself					What 3 words describe you?		
2	What to you want to create at school? Problem to solve?		400 words					
2	What do you do for fun?		400 words					
2	How do you contribute to our diversity?		400 words					
2	How do you define a successful college experience?			300 words				
3	Tell us something we didn't ask about you.			300 words				
1	Talk about experience with inclusivity							
1	Tell us about something that went wrong.							
1	Describe a problem you solved.							
1	Why STEM career?		3 examples, 120 words each					
1	How will you help shape the school community?							
1	What school readings have you enjoyed?				200 words, listed			
1	What reading outside of school do you enjoy?				200 words, listed			
1	List websites, journals, podcasts you enjoy				200 words, listed			
1	List movies, lectures, etc. at school you enjoyed				200 words, listed			
1	List other activities we should know about.							
1	How did you spend last 2 summers							
1	What historical event would you want to have witnessed?							
1	What is a new skill you would like to learn in college?							
1	What brings you joy?							
1	What song represents the soundtrack of your life at this moment?							

Harvard U	Harvey Mudd	MIT	Princeton U	Rensselaer Polytechnic Institute	Stanford U	UCSD	UC Berkeley	U Penn	Vanderbilt
Y/N	Y/N	Y/N	Y/N	Y/N	Y/N	Y/N	Y/N	Y/N	Y/N
Yes	Yes		Yes	Yes	Yes			Yes	Yes
				Resume				Resume	Resume
Yes		Yes	Yes		Yes			Yes	
3	0	7	7	2	8	4	0	4	1
					250 words	250 - 350 words		450 words	
			250 words, Why Engineering at Princeton?	250 words					
		100 words						650 words	
150 words (elaborate on 1 activity)			150 words (elaborate on 1 activity)	300 words (1 activity)	250 words	250 - 350 words			
		250 words	250 words		50 words (1 extracurricular example)	250 - 350 words			400 words (1 example)
		250 words			250 words (note to your future roommate)	250 - 350 words			
					50 words (biggest problem in society today?)				
		250 words							
		150 words							
					50 words (1 thing you look forward to at Stanford)				
No word limit stated		500 words, Common App essay							
			250 words						
		250 words							
								250 words	
								200 words	
150 words									
					50 words				
					50 words				
			50 words						
			50 words						
			50 words						

Show up on time

Whenever possible, fitting it in with your other responsibilities and commitments, block out times in advance for focused work on your applications. Play music in the background if you desire (preferably instrumental, without distracting vocals) but otherwise remove distractions. It turns out that multitasking makes people less productive, not more productive on producing quality work, so set up a conducive environment to slog through the process.

Use a CRM to manage your opportunities

There's a meaningful difference between thinking about doing something and writing out what that something to do is, particularly for a busy, overworked person such as yourself. When you have your to-do list items and deadlines stored in your mind, they probably swirl around with all the other noise in your head. Or you can organize them in a management system. I find it best to treat my big personal aspirations like any important professional project, and try to plan them out accordingly to ensure continued progress.

I've used Hubspot's free version of its Customer Relationship Management (CRM) tool to list, organize, prioritize, and track progress on a range of personal and professional projects. I find it helpful in ensuring tasks or project elements do not fall through the cracks, and it is also reminding me to follow up on longer-term projects. CRM software is typically used by companies to manage clients and sales opportunities, where each opportunity is moved along a process from, say, initial customer contact to sales presentation to pricing proposal to ultimately approval or decline by the customer.

For our purposes, it can be used to organize our different ideas, initiatives, pursuits, aspirations, and proposals. For example, if you are seeking to exhibit your artwork in formal venues, you could use a CRM to individually list prospective galleries or shows you would like to consider, set timelines or deadlines for each opportunity, and track your progression. The objective is to keep moving your projects further along the path to completion. Hopefully you are able to move each opportunity toward successful acceptance, but if you get declined, that's fine, mark it as such to remove it from your priority list (unless you want to go back and re-apply), and continue focusing on the active opportunities. One nice thing about using a CRM in this way is it helps make rejection not feel so personal. By listing and prioritizing all your prospective pursuits in a CRM pipeline, it helps visualize how many opportunities are available to you to pursue (which are probably more than you initially realize). Didn't get accepted into one show? Keep pushing the other opportunities forward. And continue adding more prospective opportunities as you find them so you maintain an active, ongoing flow of opportunities for your art. Or your music, research, coding, work, or whatever you want to get better at doing.

A CRM is valuable for you being able to hold yourself accountable for the goals you choose to set, meaning that if you tell yourself you'd like to pursue a particular opportunity, pitch, proposal, whatever, then it is up to you to see that effort to completion. A positive result allows you to continue forward, and a negative result or decline allows you to redirect yourself toward other opportunities that will be a better use of your time and effort. You should consider your CRM a long-term asset you can use to keep you on track for your larger aspirations. It is a helpful tool to review on an on-going basis to remind you of tasks you might have started a while ago and should follow up on. As life gets in the way and you get distracted elsewhere, returning to your CRM after weeks or even months can refocus you toward your big goals.

A CRM can be used specifically for your college application processing but that may be overkill as the application process itself is generally similar for each college. You can use it as a to-do manager so you feel good by checking tasks off your list, but by now I have a feeling you know the application processing drill.

Another resource that enables you to get highly granular on projects is Trello, which allows you to break projects down into discrete tasks. The interface is easy to use, and is a resource that is intended for project managers. Trello is a powerful tool for projects well beyond your application process, and can be used for many different personal and professional purposes.

An added benefit of learning how to work with tools such as HubSpot and Trello is gaining familiarity with "adult" working tools, which makes you incrementally more competent at managing projects, which is always a good skill to develop.

Chapter 8 – Become Subject Matter Knowledgeable

In a December 12, 2007 interview, the comedian, author, actor, and musician Steve Martin was asked by the host, Charlie Rose, what advice he would give to people who want to become successful. Steve said (edited for clarity), "Well it really is this: when people ask me, 'How do you make it in show business?' what I always tell them – I've said it many years and nobody ever takes note of it because it's not the answer they want it to hear – what they want to hear is 'Here's how you get an agent,' 'Here's how you write a script,' 'Here's how you do this,' but I would say **Be so good they can't ignore you**. I just think that if somebody's thinking *How can I be really good?* people are going to come to you. It's much easier than doing it that way than going to cocktail parties."[3]

At any point in your life – high school included – it's healthy and, hopefully, invigorating to remain curious and open to considering new information, meaning, and perspectives to both broaden and deepen your foundation of knowledge. If you are learning more about something you agree with, it can help you become more articulate in that field. If it's a topic you disagree with (say, for example, the argument that the Earth is flat), understanding the mindset that drives such a belief can help with entering into constructive conversation. Recognize that understanding is not the same as accepting, and I hope you use your knowledge for good to advance, uplift, and empower others.

When I talk about developing deep knowledge, I use the phrase "become subject matter knowledgeable" as opposed to "become a subject matter expert" since it's not appropriate for most people to self-describe as an expert. That's for others to decide and it also puts undue pressure on an aspiring learner to reach a goal rather than embrace the knowledge journey.

In high school, a large part of your "job" is to attend class and learn about the subjects you signed up for, take tests, get measured against your peers, and move on at the end of the semester. That is fine and keep up the good work. For your personal growth and satisfaction, consider looking far beyond the boundaries of your high school bubble to explore and engage in the big wide world more. Much more.

To me, it does not matter what the topic is, but to you it should be something that you're curious about. Too often, adults (and admissions boards) ask what you are "passionate" about, which can be a difficult question to answer because it's so final, suggesting there's no flexibility in your interest(s) to alter course or pivot or simply stop pursuing. Obviously you can and should have

---

[3] Martin, Steve, "Charlie Rose Interview - Steve Martin," YouTube.com, n.d., https://www.youtube.com/watch?v=teAvv6jnuXY.

multiple interests, whatever they may be. You may encounter societal or peer pressure to either focus in certain areas or pressure to not pursue what you really want. Ultimately, the decision should be yours. Advocate for yourself as needed.

The list of "interests" you can consider is infinite. (Not sure if it's literally or figuratively infinite, but it is nevertheless infinite). Whether it's biotechnology, artificial intelligence, human rights, arts, finance, poetry, or even chronicling The Simpsons cartoon universe, learn about what interests you. An important aspect of doing things your own way is charting a bespoke path that is logical and suited for you but challenging {or nigh impossible} for others to duplicate. One challenge in doing so, ideally, is that you should feel naturally drawn and enticed into your interest rather than forcing yourself to develop curiosity. Your time is precious, you're busy, and college applications are looming so be conscientious about managing these opposing forces.

The good news is, when you want to learn something for learning's sake, knowledge can accumulate quickly and stick in your brain, as opposed to having to study and memorize your mandated coursework. So don't despair – you can become subject matter knowledgeable faster than you might expect.

So what? Why does this matter? If you become subject matter knowledgeable but don't do anything with that knowledge, it probably does not matter much. If you use your powers and knowledge for good; however, you can make yourself unstoppable. In other chapters we'll discuss how to make use of your particular subject matter knowledge (whatever that might be) so for now, let's focus on opening the world to your curious mind.

Pay Attention

"You see, but you do not observe. The distinction is clear," Sherlock Holmes once said to Dr. John Watson. "For example, you have frequently seen the steps which lead up from the hall to this room."

"Frequently," Watson replied.

"How often?"

"Well, some hundreds of times."

"Then how many are there?" Holmes asked.

"How many? I don't know."

"Quite so! You have not observed. And yet you have seen. That is just my point. Now, I know that there are seventeen steps, because I have both seen and observed."

Although Holmes would likely be a professor most students would avoid, he had a point.

I once heard a story about a young adult who was interviewing for an office job at a large company. On their resumé, the candidate listed they previously worked at a McDonald's as an in-store staff member. The interviewer asked the candidate for more information about that job. Now, from interviews I've conducted, I would have expected a candidate to say they worked on the food preparation line or rang up orders at the cashier – which that candidate also did – and those types of responses are often said with a lack of enthusiasm and sometimes even unwarranted embarrassment. (Always remember there is dignity in any job well done.) Instead, that candidate answered, "McDonald's has one of the best supply chains in the world. Every night at closing each store knows exactly how many hamburger buns will be needed for the next day, and every morning that number of buns gets delivered. It was a fantastic learning environment for me…"

Wow.

Not what I would have expected to hear from a young interviewee and an excellent answer, which arguably any of that candidate's McDonald's co-workers could have said as well. But they probably did not because they might not have observed what the candidate saw, even though they were in the same environment. Furthermore, the candidate was able to articulate what they observed in a manner that illustrated curiosity and a desire to learn. There is tremendous value in being able to see what others do not.

Time is either invested or spent. If you are working at a retail store, pay attention to how it runs so you could be qualified to manage the store, don't just clock in and clock out. The same goes for any other activity you are doing. Now, the onus will be on you to dig deeper into your surroundings, as your co-workers and supervisor may not care to "distract" themselves by explaining things to you outside your job description. That's to be expected and that creates opportunity for you to become bigger, since those limitations for learning will apply to those around you as well.

If you are the type of person who can pay attention to what's going on around you, and even what's beneath the surface of the obvious, that would suggest you possess natural curiosity. You can also practice and get better at being observant, which I believe reinforces natural curiosity. It's a healthy habit to develop and a healthy attitude to carry.

Curated news

To continually push your self-directed education, it's important to proactively seek valid information. In high school, students are spoon-fed what to learn: use this textbook, read this article, watch these documentaries. In your larger learning, you have to go out and seek knowledge, ensuring you have a continual stream of accurate, relevant, applicable, and hopefully actionable information coming your way that you can absorb and retain.

Reading newspapers and magazines sometimes feels like a dying art, but the importance of doing so should not be ignored. In our short-attention span world, reading longform journalism is a healthy habit to work into your brain space. Also, college applications (such as Columbia University) will sometimes ask what newspapers and magazines you read regularly so that is a good motivator to do so as well. It also may help you become a better conversationalist. If you want to study and perform music, for instance, in addition to practicing your technical skills on your chosen instrument, you should also broaden your perspective on not only your art but your industry and pay attention to what's being covered in *Music Industry Weekly, Music Week, Billboard, Gramophone*, or other behind-the-scenes industry insider sources to provide broader context and perspective the same way working professionals likely do. You do not have to subject yourself to a proverbial firehose of information coming at you constantly, rather you should strive to ensure you are receiving enough quality insights and news to keep you current and articulate on your areas of interest.

Trickle-feed your learning

I'm a big proponent of subscribing to quality industry newsletters, blogs, and other sources of useful subject matter getting delivered to my email inbox on a regular basis. I don't necessarily need to read them all, sometimes only scanning the headlines and other times going in depth, but these sources of information keep me current on developments and activities in my diverse fields of interest. Often, when I'm exploring a new topic, I might subscribe to numerous email newsletters to receive a steady data dump to familiarize myself with the space. Over time I'll likely unsubscribe from the sources that are lower value or less informative for my purposes. There is an overabundance of free signups as publishers want to grow their followers so there's no reason not to initially subscribe.

Whatever your subject, a valuable aspect of these sources of information is that they are current and should give perspective on what's happening in the wider world, not just curated for high schoolers. Over time (and it might be quick), you can get familiar with understanding industry jargon, organizations, influences, and influencers. Perspective broadened.

For example, if you are interested in writing and getting published eventually, subscribing to the *Publisher's Weekly* newsletter makes sense, or *Business Week* for finance, or *Wired Magazine* for tech developments. Even if your interest is a random hobby (perhaps Parkour) or some form of unstructured recreation (for instance, sea glass collecting), there are most certainly sources of information and newsfeeds somewhere out there to feed your curiosity, you just have to make the minor effort to search online.

Turbocharge your learning

Let's face it, on balance, most every high-performing student's academic transcript generally looks the same. After all, there are only so many classes every high school offers so there are only so many advanced classes and APs one can take. Those classes would be expected on a transcript nowadays so they are a standard, not an exception, for competitive universities. Sorry, but it's true.

While you are still in high school, I strongly recommend you look at online courses through Coursera, EdX, Udemy, LinkedIn Learning, or any of the many other sites that offer advanced learning in whatever you may be interested in. Obtaining certificates of completion when available is an added benefit to demonstrate you took the course seriously and to completion. On your resumé, it speaks well to show that you've put the time and effort into learning over and above your standard school curriculum. What I find personally satisfying about these offerings is that can be highly specific to a topic, providing deep insight into a facet of what interests you. Some courses are brief, others may last weeks or months so determine what works for you and your other obligations. The objective here is not to simply accumulate certificates or bullet points for your resumé, but to absorb and retain the knowledge. Application reviewers can likely tell if courses are being listed for window dressing (such as when a plethora of courses are taken in a short timeframe at the beginning of Senior year). To continue your subject matter knowledge growth, aim to continue taking courses continually as your time allows.

Certificates versus certifications

A certificate is a document that verifies you completed a course, meeting some type of grading requirement. A certificate is not the same as a typical academic degree. A certification is a professional credential that is earned through structured training or testing, and indicates the bearer has a certain level of training or expertise in their field. Certifications are typically higher in credential than a certificate.

When available for online or in-person courses, I am partial to obtaining certificates of completion as demonstration that you did the work. Although most courses on Coursera and EdX are free, you can obtain a certificate for an additional fee. Coursera charges $50 for a certificate and EdX charges $100 (they say $99 but we know that's $100 in practical terms). These certificates do not count toward any academic credit, but they can be additive to note it on resumés and in LinkedIn profiles as an indication of your commitment to learn.

Certifications are valuable in demonstrating your commitment and interest in your field. Whether it's a Red Cross Lifeguard Certification, (ISC)[2] Certified in Cybersecurity Certification, or Google Digital Garage's range of certifications, going over and above your high school requirements will broaden your capabilities and, in turn, your horizons.

So what?

To pursue your outside-of-high-school interests, your time is limited and to develop subject matter knowledge you will have be selective in how and where you direct yourself. It's not uncommon for individuals to go down "rabbit holes" or into tangential directions that stray from their primary objective, essentially getting unproductively sidetracked. It's a good habit to do regular self-checks on your progression to ensure you continue to point yourself in your intended direction. As I conduct research on different topics that are new to me, I have found it valuable and constructive to ask myself "So what?" as I work, meaning "Is this direction of inquiry relevant and additive to my objective?" Sometimes it's not, and by pausing to check where I am headed I am able to redirect my focus back toward my main research direction.

Learn what you need to get the job done

As you develop your knowledge, you should seek opportunities to hone your skills in practical, applicable ways. For example, if you are curious about conducting college-level (or higher) research but do not know what standard researchers are held to, through Coursera.com the University of London and SOAS University of London offer a course in Understanding Research Methods[4], which outlines the fundamentals of doing research, aimed primarily, but not exclusively, at the postgraduate level. This is a free Massive Open Online Course (MOOC). According to the description, the course is designed to last four weeks and require 10 to 15 hours; however, in practical terms the course materials include an estimated 70 minutes of reading materials, a total of 40 minutes of videos to watch, and four writing assignments that may require up to one hour each. If a student wanted to learn the material as quickly as possible, this course could be completed in less than one day and still at a constructive pace where much of if the information could be retained and mentally catalogued by the student.

Is it worthwhile to earn a certificate in this topic? Maybe, if you are seeking to demonstrate to sponsors or other researchers that you are genuinely interested in working at a peer-reviewed level of research. If you desired to take the course for your own education so you can become better informed and more articulate on the topic, then you can achieve that without a certificate. Either way, the goal here is you to come away materially smarter on the subject than when you started as another step to build upon.

---

[4] Dr. J. Simon Rofe, "Understanding Research Methods - University of London," Coursera, n.d., https://www.coursera.org/learn/research-methods.

Membership Societies

Associating and collaborating with like-minded individuals, including subject matter experts, can lead to unexpected opportunities to further your knowledge, capabilities, and credentials. Consider if there are academic, professional, or social organizations that would expand your reach.

For example, I am a Fellow at the Explorers Club, which promotes research, conservation, and exploration of the natural world (land, sea, air, space) and personally the club's activities both remind and encourage me that there's so much of the Earth left for me to discover. Through their journals and magazine I gain exposure to research, expeditions, and adventures other members are pursuing. The club has fed my longstanding fascination with Antarctica and I continually learn through my membership. The society, like many others, allows students to apply for membership and get involved.

The Royal Geographic society in the UK is another such organization promoting the advancement of exploration and geographic interests. In every discipline, there are likely societies that see to promote advancement of their field. The Mathematics Association of America, which strives to advance the understanding of mathematics and its impact on our world accepts student members as well. And the list goes on.

Student membership dues are typically less expensive than standard memberships, which should make participation more affordable. In these types of groups, you'll get out of it what you put into it. Depending on the organization, a student may be defined as someone who is currently in college or university, others may allow high school-age students to join. Be open-minded as you search for societies that may be of interest to you. If you find one that you really want to participate in but don't meet the stated criteria, it never hurts to contact the organizers and ask if there's flexibility for you to join. If the answer is No, you can always apply once you qualify in the future. Remember that your continuing education is a long-term pursuit and don't let yourself get discouraged by any temporary setbacks you may encounter.

Sometimes a group may require endorsement by one or two current members. If you are interested in joining but don't know any members, oftentimes you can contact the club organizers to express your interest and ask for their help in introducing you to members local to your region who may be willing to connect with you and sponsor your application.

There are also societies where everyone is welcome to join, such as the USA Jigsaw Puzzle Association, so if you're looking for your particular tribe, it's most likely out there waiting for you.

Once you are accepted in, you can choose to be a more passive member and stay up-to-date on information, you can get actively involved in projects and initiatives, or you could choose to do nothing and merely add it as a line item for your resumé. Whatever works best for you is fine, but I would press that last option of joining just to appear impressive is wasted opportunity and wasted money.

Be wary of college enrichment courses

There are an abundance of impressive-sounding summer programs offered to high school students by countless colleges and universities across the U.S. and internationally, often offered by the brand-name institutions aspiring applicants want to gain acceptance to. Many are competitively selective and based on merit, whereas others appear to be expensive programs that are geared more toward generating easy revenue for the schools. Explore these options carefully. I believe there is value in taking summer courses that earn college credit. I am less of a fan of programs that sell softer goals such as experiencing life in a college dormitory or sitting passively in some college-level lectures. Understandably, it's highly tempting to participate in any program offered by a top school as a quick credential. I recommend discerning between the two types of opportunities before spending what may likely be several thousands of dollars on any program. Your parents will thank you.

Workshops and hands-on learning

When the opportunity arises, consider participating in in-person or online presentations or workshops that can advance your skills and understanding. Whether it runs an hour, a single day, or several days, a good workshop led by seasoned industry practitioners can rapidly advance a participant's skillset. I find them encouraging to keep pushing my work forward.

For example, for aspiring writers, the OpEd Project, which seeks to "elevate the ideas and knowledge of underrepresented expert voices, including women, and to accelerate solutions to the world's biggest problems – problems that cannot be solved justly or sustainably without a diversity of voices, expertise, experience and identity,"[5] offers online workshops on writing effectively and impactfully to promote change. They offer needs-based scholarship and welcome people with or without publishing experience.

---

[5] "The OpEd Project," n.d., https://www.theopedproject.org/.

Chapter 9 – Impersonate an Adult

We all live in our own bubble. Some people's bubbles are larger than others. Make yours as large and as interesting as possible. Whenever and however possible, you should strive to think beyond the high school bubble you are inhabiting and venture out into the larger world beyond, navigating under your own captainship.

Most high schoolers are programmed to ask for permission from authorities to be allowed to do things they desire to do. Parents, teachers, coaches, whomever. And I've found most adult authorities to be either woefully unimaginative, too busy to get involved, too trepidatious to let the young person take risks, or some combination of all these. And that's fine in most circumstances. But you are not most high schoolers.

If you are seeking to advance your craft meaningfully and impactfully, get comfortable with the concept that you will need to engage and interact with practitioners and professionals in your desired field on a growing basis. While that may sound intimidating, do recognize that your development will likely be a series of small, cumulative steps that propel you forward.

Being the youngest person in the room might trigger different emotions in different people. One person might dread that realization, convincing themselves they are unqualified or even unworthy to be included. Another might relish being able to participate in a situation that is otherwise off-limits to most people their age. A third person might not consider their age as a relevant factor in their ability to contribute constructively to the environment. Whatever situation you find yourself in, do try to remind yourself that if you are in the room, it's because for some reason or other you earned the right to be there. You can continue to be worthy of that privilege by seeking to be a neutral to positive contributor to the situation.

Conferences, conventions, and industry events

We're discussing conferences, conventions, and industry events in this chapter (as opposed to the previous chapter on developing subject matter knowledge) because this strategy requires you to be an active participant rather than a more passive learner. Meaning, you will have to talk to strangers, which understandably may not be high up on your list of most comfortable things to do but once you get used to doing so, these can be precious opportunities to learn.

One meaningful way for a candidate to separate themselves from other high school students is to engage in serious activities meant for grownups. Whatever your area of interest might be, there are opportunities such as industry conferences (in-person or virtual), tradeshows, talks, performances, exhibits or other types of participatory events that would be eye-opening and informative to advance your craft and help develop deeper subject matter knowledge. Opportunities are cumulative so you should strive to become better rounded continually, broadening your perspective with every step. Besides being personally fulfilling, these situations can make for excellent talking points to demonstrate how actively interested you are in a subject or issue.

Obtaining access to some industry events can be challenging, and that's what makes it even more distinctive for you to be there, participating and engaging with other curious, serious-minded people. (I use the word "industry" loosely here, referring to any field of interest.) Depending on the circumstances, you might need to convince your parent or other adult to register for an event and include you. Or you can register for a student ticket (which might be intended for college students but might allow flexibility). Other times, I've found that a well-written email to the event organizers may help a high school student gain access, particularly if you have ability to write an article about the event for either your high school paper or some other outlet (we'll discuss much more on publishing in *Chapter 12 – Create Information and Generate Deliverables*).

Some industry events require expensive tickets to enter (since an attendee's company would usually pay the cost) so those events would likely fall outside what many parents are willing to pay, but there are always other event opportunities that are free or affordable if you search carefully enough. Again, what makes participating in industry events notable (whatever your area of interest) is that so many other high schoolers don't, won't, or can't pursue these opportunities.

One of my daughters is an avid artist and photographer and we have attended the annual PhotoPlus Expo in New York City multiple times. It's a large industry event with free tickets where much of the best products, tech, and techniques are on display for visitors to try out. It's a fantastic learning opportunity for both of us to keep our skills current, collect a lot of fun vendor freebies, and, most importantly, learn. What's more, my daughter -- who brings her digital camera with her – has been able to spend meaningful time taking studio photos of professional models, using professional lighting setups provided by the exhibitors showcasing their product lines. This has enabled her to add several stunning, magazine-quality images of professional models to her photo portfolio, which she has since included in her portfolio submissions. She has also gained exposure to understanding the way working professionals advance their craft and make a living.

In another situation, I took a person to a leading cybersecurity conference in Washington DC, where we attended talks and panel discussions by industry experts and government leaders of intelligence agencies (i.e., spies) on cyber threats around the world, digital solutions, and industry outlooks on what's coming next. In addition to the first-hand insights we were hearing from working professionals, being exposed to that community was fascinating and highly educational. Both of us deepened our subject matter knowledge and ability to articulate complex topics in a credible manner. Plus it was just plain fun.

To be taken seriously at these events, or at least not stand out awkwardly, remember to dress and carry yourself like an adult. It's a good rule of thumb to be dressed slightly better than your audience, wherever you might be, so proper business attire is the safe bet. And no sneakers. For more creative, less business or academic, situations, figure out what the norm and determine how best to fit in. On the event websites there are often photos of past events so you can gauge the room.

When you do attend events, I recommend making the effort to speak with vendors and exhibitors (which typically requires high schoolers to step waaaaaay out of their comfort zone). It's okay to ask thoughtful questions, or pick up literature and brochures if they seem interesting. Just don't interrupt people mid-conversation. These situations are good practice to tamp down the nervous awkward feelings that often accompany serious public gatherings. Learn to develop your inner peace in public. In a small yet cumulative way, these conversations with a serious stranger may give you some practice for the one-on-one interviews you'll eventually be doing with your college application interviewers.

Learn from industry practitioners about their craft

Be on the lookout for opportunities where you can gain exposure to practitioners demonstrating their craft and try to learn from their praxis [another good SAT word for you. If you don't already know what it means, look it up]. Either in-person or online, there's valuable benefit learning how respected people in your field talk about their work, their philosophy, their methods, what they demand of themselves, and what support they may seek from others. Artist talks, panel discussions, lectures, interviews, OpEd articles, documentaries, biographies, and autobiographies are examples of the myriad of opportunities to learn from people who have forged paths ahead of you. If you pay attention, hopefully you will glean aspects that you may choose to emulate and – equally importantly – recognize aspects that you decide are not suitable for your personal praxis.

Open mic nights

I applaud anyone who has the intestinal fortitude to perform on stage. Whether school performances or other formal opportunities, congratulations for putting yourself out there. For people who do not have the opportunity to be part of an organized performance, performing at open mic nights or the equivalent for your art offers potentially more opportunities to perform. A wealth of different experiences would be acquired throughout that process, from researching events and opportunities, committing to perform, preparing material, arranging logistics to the venue, performing, all the way through to the post-performance spectrum of emotions.

Public events

Get yourself out there. Seek events such as art gallery exhibit openings, site tours, and other opportunities outside of the typical high school bubble most people your age populate. Do.

Chapter 10 – Advocate for Yourself

"Well-behaved women seldom make history."
                                                    Laurel Thatcher Ulrich[6]

Learning how to advocate for yourself in the "adult" world is different than learning how to ask for permission. I view self-advocacy as seeking collaboration, partnership, information sharing, or other manner of exploration to advance a cause. Talk is easy, action takes work. To get what you want regarding your larger aspirations, you will have to become your own strongest advocate and break through that sometimes real, sometimes imaginary barrier that separates you from the larger world of opportunities.

Asking permission is "Would it be okay if I go to your exclusive event…" whereas advocating would be more along the lines of "I would like to support your important work at your event by…"

Being able and willing to ask for help or guidance, pitch your ideas, present your credentials, being taken seriously, gaining access to suitable events, even writing a compelling cover letter are all important skills that can be learned.

Broaden your perspective

While you are trying to figure yourself out and come up with a plan on how you can fit better in the adult world, it's important to recognize that many adults are still trying to do so as well. And many have been trying for years or even decades as adults. Most of us are still trying to figure it out so hopefully that makes everything I propose below a little less intimidating.

Learn how to pitch

I am not your bro, your bruv, your homeboy, your bud or buddy. Until I allow otherwise, I'm Mr. Huang to you if you are contacting me for the first time. Using a proper form of address also applies to anyone else you may be contacting for the first time, and until such time as they either explicitly say, "Call me Ishmael" or sign off with their first name. Use proper forms of address as a sign of

---

[6] A lot of women are credited with this quote, but Laurel Thatcher Ulrich was the originator, written when she was a PhD student, and is a nice reminded of how everyone can leave their own mark. "Well-Behaved Women Seldom Make History," QuoteInvestigator.com, n.d., https://quoteinvestigator.com/2012/11/03/well-behaved-women/.

respect. You'd be surprised at how many people don't start with that simple courtesy, which – since you always will – will give you an ever-so-slight advantage as a well-mannered individual. The rule applies whether you are writing to someone or meeting them in person for the first time. And for the next few years you should seek to apply it to both formal and informal first meetings as a way of showing courtesy.

Not too long ago I went to my local grocery store and a local group had set up a table and display near the front entrance for some sort of fundraiser. Two grown men were manning the table, casually dressed, and lingering about. As I walked toward the entrance, one of them called out, "Hey bro." I smiled and acknowledged his presence as I went into the store. It struck me how sloppy the man's approach was. His clothes were sloppy to begin with, and his lack of courtesy rubbed me the wrong way. Clothes don't have to be expensive or any particular style, but you can tell when someone may hold themselves to a personal standard of care and dignity. And you can tell when they do not. His demeanor made me actively not want to spend the time to hear their pitch, since I (correctly or incorrectly, I'll never know) assumed they were equally sloppy with how they'd handle donations. Imagine if he made the effort to say, "Good afternoon." First of all, it would have caught me off guard, and would also impel me to pause and return more of measured, engaged greeting in return.

Mr., Ms., Mrs., Mx.

Acknowledging and respecting preferred pronouns can be challenging unless the person you'd like to contact explicitly provided their pronouns somewhere. Rather than use a "Mr." or "Ms.", I'm testing out the neutral "Mx." on correspondence. I haven't yet decided if that will be my go-to format but have not found a more effective alternative for blind solicitations yet.

Definitely gonna give you up

"Gonna" is not a word, so don't use it when you are going to write to someone, even if only in an email. The same goes for "ain't."

Use "going to" and "is/am/are not."

Learn how to write a cover letter

From personal experience, I'm amazed at how much good can result from sending out a well-written letter. Most high schoolers have not had many opportunities to send out cover letters or pitch letters. When you get used to doing so you will have a meaningful advantage in asking for opportunities. I continue to be amazed (and gratified) at how a well-written email can open doors for students. You can see an example of one that worked for one of my students seeking an internship below.

When an internship or job posting requires a cover letter, without providing an addressee, it's fairly common to address the letter as "Dear [Company name] hiring manager:", which is terribly inelegant and impersonal, but that seems to be the default approach. I'm still looking for something better.

If you are contacting a company with multiple office locations and you are not specifically referring to one location, it's best to use the headquarters address in your letter. Sending a cover letter PDF electronically (as opposed to filling in a form field on an application) looks more professional when you include a proper mailing address.

Nothing ventured, nothing gained

By pursuing some or all of the recommendations in this book you will most certainly be a more interesting teenager than the general population. Become subject matter knowledgeable, read, listen, learn about whatever field you might have an interest in and then network and lean on your network's network for ideas and introductions.

"No way that's going to work," you might be thinking. If you believe it won't work, you're right. For everyone else reading this; however, here's one situation I helped a student with:

Rebecca [by the way, all real names have been changed in this book] had been taking online computer science classes for over a year and was particularly excited to learn about cybercrime. She listened avidly to a popular cybercrime podcast and found the stories fascinating, eye-opening, and inspirational should she ever go to the dark side. We played with the idea of how valuable and informative it would be to be a research intern for that leading podcast so we wrote a clear and concise email to the host. The credentials listed below are Rebecca's actual credentials, but anonymized somewhat for privacy.

The subject was straightforward, "Dear Mr. Henry, I want to be your intern"

The cover letter said:

Dear Mr. Henry:

I am writing to express my very strong interest in supporting [Podcast name]'s important work as an intern. I am currently a high school senior and intending to pursue a cyber security degree at university. I have a diverse educational and professional background, which I believe is highly relevant, and I respectfully present my credentials for your consideration.

I recently completed an internship with the Cybersecurity and Communication Integration Cell, a division of Homeland Security, which is my State's authority on cybersecurity information sharing, threat analysis, and incident reporting. My work included researching into a wide range of threat tools, tactics, and procedures, and exploring strategies to counter malicious cyberattacks.

I am also an Editorial Board Member of [a women-oriented media outlet's youth division], which supports media and leadership training as well as advocacy campaigns. As a monthly contributor, I write articles to raise awareness of pressing issues affecting young people, including my 2021 article, "Internet Safety Tips for Teens."

Additionally, I am co-authoring the book, "Fundamental Cyber Security for Everybody – 2022 Edition," scheduled for publication in November 2021, where I provide pragmatic instruction on personal digital resilience, such as protecting oneself from SIM swapping, spearphishing, and social media hijacking.

At my high school, I am currently a senior pursuing my International Baccalaureate degree. Outside of school. I have completed several cyber and programming courses, including Artificial Intelligence with Python with Harvard University summer school; Convoluted Neural Networks, Improving Deep Neural Networks: Hyperparameter Tuning, Regularization and Optimization, Structural Machine Learning Projects, and Neural Networks and Deep Learning with DeepLearning.ai; and also Machine Learning Operations Fundamentals with Google Cloud / Coursera.

Outside of my technical work, I am also an independent humanitarian advocate actively focused on the Global Refugee Crisis. I have documented the on-the-ground situation in refugee camps across Greece and Mexico, and have presented my findings through two TEDx Talks, articles, university lectures, and gallery and museum exhibits. A larger part of my value comes from my ability to identify unconventional solutions to challenges, combined with independent thinking and a proclivity for crafting entrepreneurial, actionable strategies for solving problems.

Attached please find my resumé to provide a detailed sense of my interests. Thank you very much in advance for your consideration and I look forward to hearing back from you.

Sincerely yours,

Rebecca Andrews

The email was a brief cover letter where Rebecca expressed her admiration for Mr. Henry's work and the podcast, her computer science and research background, her ability to be flexible for the show's needs, some of her skills (including research, writing, editing, and marketing), and she attached her properly formatted resumé.

Within a couple of days, she received an email back from the host requesting a phone interview. She was hired and now does remote research for shows to be produced. It has created an excellent opportunity for Rebecca to conduct research into great stories, become a journalist, learn about the production process, and learn how to write and edit scripts and copy.

All because of a well-written email, independently-obtained subject matter knowledge, and the boldness to ask.

Another student, Pasqual, was also interested in computer science and had taken several online courses on his own time. He wanted to gain experience and leveraged his circle of relationships to have an adult ask a friend if that friend's company (a global technology consulting firm) could use a high school intern. The answer was Yes, and Pasqual did 6 weeks, 20 hours a week in an unpaid summer internship learning how to develop an AI platform for managing legal documents, and designing programs to process digital files. All because he was willing to ask. Also, he was willing to ask for introductions from his extended network of family, friends, and their extended relationships. It was real-world experience creating demanding deliverables for his boss's client.

An internship is not required for you to be successful, and may not suit everybody. A real internship in a grownup setting can be a highly distinctive opportunity to differentiate yourself from the competition. Granted, the biggest hurdle a high schooler will likely face is that they have no skills, no knowledge, and often no clue. But you are going to ensure that doesn't describe you.

Collect rejections

Further to the benefits of writing a compelling pitch, success is built on a series of rejections. Embrace the idea that ongoing success is built on ongoing rejections. For your mental well-being, never take rejection as a negative. It's counter-intuitive but when you get rejected you usually have two choices: go back and ask a second time or redirect your efforts to somewhere more fruitful. Either choice may be appropriate depending on the situation. If you are determined, remember that many other people simply stop at No and move no further, so repitching may be worthwhile. If you do decide the answer truly is No then move on quickly with no regrets and no hard feelings.

Leave a mark

Soon after their return, a letter was delivered to Miss Bennet; it came from Netherfield, and was opened immediately. The envelope contained a sheet of elegant, little, hot pressed paper, well covered with a lady's fair, flowing hand...

Pride and Prejudice by Jane Austen

Dinner over, we produced a bundle of pens, a copious supply of ink, and a goodly show of writing and blotting paper. For there was something comfortable in having plenty of stationery.

Great Expectations by Charles Dickens

The art of letter writing is dead. Well, almost dead. Writing letters by hand is tedious. Being able to write in cursive, or script, is equally endangered. Schools have not been required to teach students how to write in cursive since 2010. When was the last time you bought postage stamps? And do you even know where your nearest mailbox is?

It's fair to assume that many of your peers are not sending out traditional correspondence on a regular basis. Most adults don't either. Sending letters requires effort. And that's the point, because receiving letters can be rare, exciting, memorable, and appreciated. Recipients recognize that the sender made an actual effort to recognize them as handwritten letter-worthy.

Writing a letter to say "Thank you" is one of the most natural opportunities to show appreciation. And it does not have to be reserved for grand gestures someone makes to you, you can (and should) thank people as often as makes sense. I always mentor my students to write Thank You notes to their hosts when invited to meaningful events, whether that may be a dinner, party, outing, or any other event where the host(s) made an effort to provide a nice experience.

Letters don't have to be Pride and Prejudice-length missives about the weather, the garden harvest, and what the neighbors wore to the local festival. They can be as long or short as necessary. Sometimes simply telling someone you were thinking of them and looking forward to seeing them again in person can be a meaningful gesture.

Nowadays we effortlessly forward online links to articles, memes, and everything else under the sun. Before the internet, people used to send article clippings or other memorabilia through the mail. If the opportunity presents itself to do something similar for individuals you value, do so. Once in a while, when I'm visiting an interesting place such as a historic site or museum I might grab an extra map and brochure if there's someone I know who might find it interesting. I'd eventually get around to sending the brochure to that person with a note saying that I enjoyed that site and thought they would too if they have a chance to visit.

Whenever anyone has taken the time and made the effort to do a similar kindness to me, it has always touched me and remains appreciatively in my memory.

As your academic and professional network increases, writing a Thank You note is an impactful way for you to be remembered. You should make it a point to write Thank You letters to people who interview you or go out of their way to share their insight or guidance.

You should also make a habit of writing at least one letter to your better and best teachers telling them you appreciate them and their efforts. If that sounds like the height of awkwardness, you can wait until the end of the course to express your appreciation. Anyway, that's what more mature, self-aware students should strive to do. It's always beneficial to develop longer-term relationships with teachers who want to see you succeed. Ideally, you can nurture relationships with mentors who know you so well that they would happily write letters of reference or recommendations for you if and when needed. Bear in mind, besides college applications, other opportunities may arise where you'll be asked to provide references or letters of recommendation so developing lasting relationships is important.

As your circle widens, you should aim to nurture relationships with mentors both during and well past your college years. You, in turn, should strive to be equally supportive of others who would benefit from your diverse wisdom and life experiences.

Order business cards, use them judiciously

Business cards are a relic of the past, before bumping phones became all it takes to share contact information. It's old school. It's archaic, even. Which is what makes it a distinctive gesture that helps people remember who you are. I'll leave it to you on the style and design since this is an opportunity for you to present your personal brand. Whatever you choose, do make sure to get them printed by a professional printshop, not on your home printer (do people still use those?) to ensure quality. Since you're younger and don't want people stopping by your home, I recommend not including your mailing address. You can include:

- Proper name – First, Middle (if desired), and Last Name, and suffixes (Jr., etc.) as needed. No Mr., Ms., Mrs., Mx. Needed.

- Pronouns – this is a personal choice; you can include your personal pronouns if it helps your purposes or omit them if not additive.

- Burner phone number – To protect your privacy, do not publicly give out your personal cellphone number. I use an alternate phone number (known as a burner number) that is linked to my cellphone number, and calls to that burner number get automatically forwarded to my phone via an easy-to-use app. Google Voice (voice.google.com) can provide you with a free alternate number to your cellphone number.

- Professional website address – if you have a website that exhibits your work, include it.

- Social media handles if appropriate – you can add your professional (not personal) social media handles if you actively use those accounts for your area of expertise.

- Email – not your personal email address, a separate professional email you setup, which can be a Gmail or other common mail service, it does not have to be a custom address, just make sure to use a professional-sounding name. You could make it your FirstnameLastname@gmail.com or reasonable variation thereof. Don't try to be funny or cute with email names, this is for your budding career.

"It was a pleasure speaking with you, would you mind if we kept in touch from time to time? I'd look forward to continuing our conversation." And politely extend your clear, crisp business card for them to accept. In turn ask if they have a business card they can provide. If they do not, see if they are willing to provide their email, phone number or some other way of connecting. Making this effort conveys to the recipient that you are a person interested in following through and who takes themselves and their work seriously.

Chapter 11 – Advocate for Others

There's nothing less imaginative in an application than listing the mandatory community service you are required to do with everyone else in your grade. If your school forces you to be benevolent and caring, if only for 2 hours, and that's the only example of you being giving of yourself, that says a lot – or is it a little? – about you and your willingness to engage in issues bigger than yourself. (Yes, I'm being cynical when I say this, but listing mandatory community service is a common weakness I find in many of my client's early drafts of applications.)

I recognize it can be intimidating offering yourself up to volunteer or to get involved with an organization. I've had conversations with students who might not feel qualified, competent, or capable enough to commit to a recurring volunteer effort. They tended to underestimate all the benefits they could bring to a worthy cause, including youth membership, technology knowledge, social media management, database skills, writing and proofreading, community outreach, energy, and a younger-person's perspective.

I do not recommend getting involved in charitable or activist causes just to have a line item on your resumé, that would be insincere and not the best use of your time. Provided you would like to get involved in advocacy or volunteer opportunities that may have lasting impact, there are endless opportunities you can explore. Many of the recommendations we will discuss to support major organizations can even be done remotely. It's well known that volunteering for causes meaningful to you is beneficial to your physical and mental health, provides a sense of purpose and teaches meaningful skills, and increases social interaction and nurtures existing and new relationships.[7]

If you have enough time before your applications are due that you can show you've made a meaningful contribution and impact to a cause, by all means share it in your application. If you don't have enough time to impact your applications but still want to volunteer your time, energy, and resources, by all means do so. Hopefully you will find the experience meaningfully satisfying and personally rewarding and want to continue participating during your college years as well.

Directories of volunteer opportunities

Opportunities to engage with causes abound if you're willing to look for them. Examples of some remote opportunities that exercise your brain muscles include:

---

[7] "3 Health Benefits of Volunteering."

VolunteerMatch

www.volunteermatch.org

VolunteerMatch is a huge database of current opportunities globally that you can search. Many organizations may have specific tasks they seek support on, such as website design, data tasks, or translation that may be suitable for your capabilities.

LinkedIn Volunteers

www.linkedin.com/jobs

You can search for volunteer opportunities through LinkedIn's job section. Add the keyword "volunteer" in your searching, and you can also filter by location or remote opportunities. LinkedIn is typically geared toward adults, but that does not preclude younger participants. Some of the opportunities may offer the "Easy Apply" option, where you click a few buttons and your LinkedIn profile is forwarded to the organization, others may require a resumé and cover letter.

Amnesty International Decoders

decoders.amnesty.org

Amnesty International campaigns to end abuses of human rights. Amnesty Decoders is an innovative platform for volunteers around the world to use their computers or phones to help Amnesty's researchers sift through pictures, information, and documents. Online training is provided before a volunteer participates in a project to ensure quality control. Their Decoders projects are diverse and have ranged from exposing online abuse faced by women politicians in India to decoding how U.S.-led bombing destroyed Raqqa, Syria, to researching oil spills in Nigeria and making oil companies accountable for devastating pollution, to finding surveillance cameras in New York City related to facial recognition technology.

For their New York City project, for example, digital volunteers were tasked with reviewing images of every intersections in New York City to identify surveillance cameras, and help reveal where people are more likely to be tracked by facial recognition technology. Using volunteers from 153 countries, a total of 45,433 locations were analyzed. The findings will be used by Amnesty in their campaign to ban facial recognition in New York.

Smithsonian Digital Volunteers

transcription.si.edu

Smithsonian Digital Volunteers help make the Smithsonian's historical documents and biodiversity data more accessible. Volunteers help transcribe and review field notes, diaries, ledgers, logbooks, currency proof sheets, photo albums, manuscripts, biodiversity specimen labels, and historic audio recordings. Because the institution's holdings are so vast and diverse, and because they have multiple transcription projects going on simultaneously, there is likely to be a project that touches on your areas of curiosity or interest.

World Youth Alliance

www.wya.org

WYA works at international institutions such as the United Nations, the European Union, and the Organization of American States, as well as with young people from around the world, seeking to build a culture that supports and nurtures the dignity of each human person. Membership is open for everyone between the ages of 10 and 30 who agree to the principles of the WYA charter. Their Certified Training Program (CTP) equips young people to communicate articulately and persuasively on behalf of the dignity of the human person. It also provides participants with a vocabulary to engage the international community and larger culture on issues relating to the dignity of the person, human rights, and integral development. WYA offer a Certified Member Track where trainees attend 7 live training discussions. Members who complete this track will be eligible to apply for the WYA internship program, to open a WYA Chapter or join a National Committee leadership team.

Carve your own Path

There is a lot to be said about grassroots activism. Taking your own initiative to create change, help others, and otherwise make the world a better and kinder place in any way can be a noble pursuit. One common challenge I have witnessed with many self-starters is a lack of staying power. I know several well-intentioned, hot-to-trot, feverishly motivated individuals who begin with a flurry of activity and enthusiasm yet burn out when the required commitment and amount of work necessary to move forward becomes taxing. Talk is easy, continuous productivity is hard. Given that, it's all the more impressive for those benevolent individuals who manage to contribute consistently to a cause, ideating, strategizing, administering, and enacting steps to help solve some of society's problems. Launching and running a charitable effort is not much different from managing a major academic or work project, and should be performed with the same level of professionalism to be effective and efficient. You can have all the best intentions going into your idea, but ultimately the results you achieve are what matter.

Join a Board

Now, recognize that it's unexpected – unreasonable even – for a high school-age person to actively participate on a not-for-profit Board. It's generally unheard of. How wonderful for You.

All organizations have some form of reporting structure. In a basic structure for a not-for-profit organization, volunteers report up to managers, managers report up to the President (or sometimes that title is Chief Executive Officer or Executive Director – whatever the title, that person is recognized as the senior-most person in charge on a day-to-day basis). The President reports up to the organization's Board. Sometimes the board is called Board of Directors, sometimes it's Board of Trustees. Either way, the Board is a group of volunteers who help guide the President (and other senior leaders) in carrying out the organization's mission, address significant issues that arise, and provide higher-level support. Individual Board members are selected for their particular skills and knowledge. There are also other types of Boards including Advisory Boards and Editorial Boards where participants contribute their skills and knowledge in a more focused manner. Board members may have opportunity to participate on different committees (an intimidating-sounding word meaning a group of individuals focused on a particular issue) such as membership, community outreach, or fundraising committees. Some Board positions may require only once-a-month or once-a-quarter (that is, once every three months) meetings, others may be meaningfully more time consuming. Each organization has their own structure, committees, and needs so you'll have to do your research into organizations that you might be interested in. Thank goodness for the About Us section of websites.

The same capabilities that you may bring to a basic volunteer position you might offer as a Board member, with more commitment on your part to contribute your capabilities to the organization's mission. Technology, social media, fundraising, and youth membership are areas where a young member can be distinctively valuable to the right Board. Ask.

Participating on an organized Board is highly educational in multiple ways, from learning firsthand how formal meetings are organized and conducted; being exposed to strategy, prioritization, and execution of initiatives; learning how to interact with adults in a formalized setting where issues are debated and decisions get made; and helping make those collective decisions.

All of the "I second that" and "Aye" and "Make a motion to…" jargon comes from Robert's Rules of Order, the basics of which can be learned easily online. Spending a few minutes to read Robert's Rules of Order can quickly demystify the confusing (and intimidating) formalities in those endless Congressional meetings you don't watch on C-SPAN.

If and when you join a Board, you should expect to be involved for at least a couple of years, this is a medium- to long-term growth and learning opportunity for you, and at the same time you develop into an increasingly valuable contributor to the organization's mission.

Chapter 12 – Create Information and Generate Deliverables

The difference between a deliverable and an idea is a deliverable is something that can be shown, shared, and showcased. Ideas float in the ether and are unproven, unmeasured, and unseen. One of the biggest challenges high school students have when applying to competitive schools is they may have worked hard all through school, did their homework diligently, and scored the scores they needed, but they don't have much to show for it in a concrete way. Links to your deliverables can also be included in resumés or applications, which always helps, provided the work you created is solid.

I'm going to provide several strategies that may help you turn your ideas into deliverables. These real-world examples should help you understand that major goals can be accomplished by taking measured, consistent steps. The procedures discussed are applicable to everyone, both high schoolers and adults, so understand these are strategies you can employ to stand on par with or even surpass most adults. The specific strategies we'll look at include:

- Public speaking,
- How to Apply to give a TEDx Talk,
- How to get an Article Published,
- How to Publish a Book Fast,
- How to Create an Online Course,
- How to Submit your Research Paper to Conferences,
- How to Exhibit your Art,
- How to get Quoted in the Media,
- How to Create a Portfolio Website, and
- How to Make your Deliverables Look, Sound, and Feel Better

Bear in mind, you can broaden these strategies to target the specific platforms, outlets, or venues most appropriate for your work. Feel free to adjust the procedures to fit your distinct objectives.

If you think you can or you can't, you are right. There are always reasons not to do something, and that's fine for most people. It's also fine to do something and it not end up working out or being as Earth-shattering as you hoped, nevertheless there can always be something to be learned. Often there are more valuable lessons to be learned from setbacks than from successes, all of which add to your foundational knowledge and panoply of experiences to make you uniquely you.

Public Speaking

Not to generalize but there are two broad types of public speakers: those who want to share an important message and those who want fame and accolades.

The former type of speaker often has solid subject matter knowledge, wants to raise awareness, or wants to mobilize action and resources to address an issue. Their goals may be to educate, inform, or motivate. [I refrain from calling them "subject matter experts" since many people can be knowledgeable and effective in sharing valuable information without being an identified "expert."] There are individuals I know who may or may not be awkward, dry, wry, or naturally charismatic, but they are fascinating to listen to because they have genuine knowledge to impart. I'll happily spend time listening to these folks any time I can.

The latter type of speaker more likely uses their platform to raise their personal visibility, social capital, and popularity. If you look on LinkedIn, there is a stratum of people who describe themselves as "keynote speaker" in their bios. I also know one individual who created a video demo reel of themselves and is a self-described Public Speaker. The rub I have with this approach is I find many of these individuals don't say what specific subject they speak about, just that for some reason they should be placed at a podium. Perhaps because they have a winning smile, or amusing anecdotes, or just yearn to be in a spotlight. It's often sizzle but no steak.

Over the years I have met both types. Be the former type. I strongly counsel people to be willing to speak up when they can educate or can help make a difference. Speak up when you can do some good for people who don't have a voice. Do not put yourself in the spotlight merely to bask in the spotlight.

Public speaking is challenging for most people, whatever their age. The difference between these two types of speakers is significant. While a person with subject matter knowledge might fumble a word, slip up on a presentation, or be met by a hostile audience, I believe their conviction in getting the information out gives them the intestinal fortitude to keep moving forward. If the audience does not like the message they're hearing, this type of speaker understands that the message is not being well received, it's not a reflection of them as a person. This speaker can get up the next day and keep waving their flag since their aim is to share information and add to the discourse on an issue.

On the other hand, if a Public Speaker seeking adoration gives a presentation and the audience isn't impressed, it is much more a rejection of the person's own qualities since to a meaningful degree their underlying aim was to obtain accolades. Ouch.

Public speaking should be about the issues, not about you. And that will make you a better public speaker.

How to Apply to Give a TEDx Talk

This idea is not for everybody, but for those who are willing to pursue them, TEDx Talks are a distinctive demonstration of subject matter knowledge.

My recommendations are based on my personal experience of giving two TEDx Talks about humanitarian issues. I have spoken to a handful of my students about considering applying to present at TEDx events. All of them said they would like to but only two individuals saw it though to successful completion.

In addition to the premiere TED Talks that are widely viewed on YouTube and TED.com, TEDx Talks are regional or local independent events that have been endorsed by the TED organization. In the spirit of TED's mission pf "ideas worth spreading," the TEDx program helps communities, organizations and individuals produce TED-style events at the local level. TEDx events are planned and coordinated independently, on a community-by-community basis, under a free license from TED. TEDx speakers are considered somewhat expert in their fields on knowledge, which may be formal knowledge or homegrown, on any topic worth socializing. Along with the headlining TED Talks, the TED organization posts TEDx Talks on TED.com and YouTube.

Giving a TEDx Talk offers several benefits to the speaker:

1. By virtue of the short format, it forces the speaker to focus on the most important aspects of their idea worth sharing.
2. It pushes the speaker to think in soundbites, which is an important skill in communications generally and especially important in public speaking.
3. It pushes the speaker to expand continually their subject matter knowledge, ensuring their Talk is as informative and relevant as possible.
4. It's an impressive credential to earn. The curators chose you because they could see you would bring value and knowledge to their audience.
5. It is one of the most terrifying yet ultimately gratifying experiences most people will have had up to that point in their lives.

Giving a TEDx Talk is possibly horrible to the speaker in certain ways:

1. The process takes at least 4 months if you are lucky and may take up to a year to complete. Depending on how close your application deadlines are, this strategy may not be viable for the purposes of a college application; however, it is still highly valuable and worthwhile for your bigger-picture aspirations, whenever you do get to give a Talk.

2. The pressure to perform is high because you'll be on stage alone, talking to a crowd of up to 100 people. But you'll get through it one way or another.

3. Imposter syndrome – the feeling like you lack the qualifications, skills, talent, or knowledge for the task at hand – is a real feeling, whether warranted or not. It's not a good feeling for anyone to experience. All the other speakers (or most at least) will seem smarter, more worldly, or more capable than you (also a normal thing to feel in these situations). Once you get through it, you'll hopefully see that you had every right to be speaking there based on the merit of your message.

4. Once you are selected to speak, it takes a lot of time to prepare so will put stress on the other parts of your life. Planning ahead is important.

The process for given a TEDx Talk include:

1. Perform a survey of the upcoming TEDx Talks to identify those that are scheduled to occur at least 3 months into the future and beyond. Curators want to identify their speakers months in advance for marketing purposes.

2. Tabulate a list of the relevant events, and methodically review their themes and speaker application requirements. Note the stated submission deadlines and response dates for all events.

3. Craft your written application responses. After you write the first application responses you should be able to recycle some or all of your answers for other applications.

4. Many applications require you to send in a brief video introduction. This is an audition tape so you should have your comments scripted in advance, looking your most presentable and professional for filming.

5. As soon as your application elements are presentation-ready, send in the applications to each event. You should apply to as many events as reasonable (that is, every event you have the logistical ability to attend). Using the cut-and-paste method of applications, I helped my students apply to approximately 15 events that spanned the upcoming 12 months.

6. Wait patiently. Tempus fugit.

7. Collect rejections. Continue to find future events where you can apply and do so. If you end up getting invited to multiple events, you can always decline one or craft different talks around your topic and give multiple talks.

8. Get accepted to an event. Celebrate.

9. Work as directed by the event producers to refine your talk, conduct rehearsals, and plan for the event date.

10. TEDx Talks are presented without notes so practice your talk repeatedly.

11. Closer to the event, participate in on-site or virtual rehearsals.
12. Day of the event – everything is an adrenaline-fueled blur. Somewhere during the day you got on stage and spoke about something.
13. End of the day – you'll likely have an adrenaline crash, crave sugar, and feel giddily exhausted.
14. Approximately 3 or more months after the event, your video should be available online on TED.com and YouTube.

If it was easy…

Below, I will give you the detailed procedures on how to do the above process because I want to set you up for success. If I glossed over the details so as not to scare you, I'd actually be setting you up for failure and that's not a good use of either of our times. Let's look at each step in detail:

1. Perform a survey of the upcoming TEDx Talks to identify those that are scheduled to occur at least 3 months into the future and beyond.
    a. Fortunately, all this information is available on TED.com. Go to TED.com > Attend > TEDx events. There you'll see a map of all upcoming events worldwide. Use the map to zoom into your region, determine how far you could reasonably travel should you be accepted. The map will show events that are open to the public and others that may be private (such as at a university) or sold out. Make note of all types as they are all opportunities to evaluate. Creating a spreadsheet can help in keeping all this information organized and prioritized.
    b. Depending on your topic or focus, consider if there's possible opportunity to apply to a talk where you'd be an outlier. For example, one of my students of Eastern European descent wanted to speak about her experiences finding her genuine voice in the United States, a great topic where she as a young person was sharing her personal observations. In addition to searching for TEDx Talks that were within her comfortable travel radius, we also looked for Talks that were scheduled around Eastern Europe, where she could propose doing a live video talk to the in-person audience. We wanted to appeal to those curators' desire for memorable speakers, and having someone present from halfway around the world with a good topic could be distinctive enough to warrant a speaker invitation.
    c. Your efforts, travel, and logistics will be self-funded, there is no funding from TEDx. Plan accordingly.
2. Tabulate a list of the relevant events, and methodically review their themes and speaker application requirements. Note the stated submission deadlines and response dates for all events.

a. Tabulate the event details – name, date, location, theme, website, application link.

b. On TED.com, clicking the TEDx event name will open the details page, which hopefully includes website and other information. Otherwise search online for details.

c. On the individual event sites, assess the theme and if there's a potential fit for your talk. Often the themes are generic – Innovation, Curiosity, The New, etc. If there is a fit, note the application deadline and, if stated by the organizers, the expected response date.

d. Go to the "Apply to Speak" page and save a copy of the application questions into a separate word processing document. You want to make the bulk application process efficient so gathering all applications and then prioritizing them will be helpful to you.

3. Craft your written application responses. After you write the first application you should be able to recycle some or all of your answers for other applications.

    a. It's important to be able to write in soundbites for these applications. Soundbites are a short sentences or phrases that are easy to remember. State the important points upfront to maintain the curators' attention.

    b. From a practical perspective, work on the application with the closest deadline first and then refine your answers as you go through iterations with other applications.

4. Many applications require you to send in a brief video introduction. This is an audition tape so you should have your comments scripted in advance, look your most presentable, and come off as someone who is professional in their work. Not only are the curators determining if you'll be good in front of their audience, they are also determining if you seem to be someone easy and professional to work with.

    a. With the soundbites you've created, craft a script for your video. You have a lot of latitude here on production style but make sure your lighting is good, you look respectable (i.e., clean, fresh, vibrant), and your background is presentable (i.e., clean, fresh, vibrant).

    b. Many event producers want your video to be personalized to their event, so would expect to hear your say, "Hello, TEDxBohemia Team, I am..." and "Hello, TEDxEllisIsland Team..." Insert the individual event name somewhere at the beginning of your script so you can easily swap names and record individual videos.

    c. Practice your script until you can recite it fairly comfortably. I am being mindful of your time here and not suggesting you memorize it in full. You can use a teleprompter app to read your script. Alternatively, you can also tape a printout of your script as close to your webcam lens as possible as a speaking aid. The closer you place the printout, the less obvious it will be that you are reading.

   d. Try to record as many individual videos as possible during the same session for efficiency. Label the video files carefully to ensure you send the correct video out to each Talk.

   e. You may be required to upload your video to YouTube. If so, make sure to set the sharing to Private, not Public. After you receive a positive or negative response from the organizers, delete them from YouTube for your security and privacy.

5. As soon as your application elements are presentation-ready, send in the applications to each event. You should apply to as many events as reasonable (that is, every event you have the logistical ability to attend). Using the cut-and-paste method of applications, my students applied to approximately 15 events that spanned the upcoming 12 months.

   a. Applying to TEDx Talks is a numbers game. Plan to send out numerous applications efficiently and in on-going waves.

6. Wait patiently. Tempus fugit.

   a. Chances are, you'll still have some incomplete applications. Strive to be thorough and continue sending out applications until you receive a positive response.

7. Collect rejections. Continue to find future events where you can apply and do so. If you end up getting invited to multiple events, you can always decline one or craft different talks around your topic and give multiple talks.

   a. Contemplate what you will be saying in your presentation. Draft ideas and a script.

8. Get accepted to an event. Celebrate.

   a. The organizers will have a detailed list of next steps for you to handle.

   b. Now you really have to think about writing your talk and creating your presentation. The organizers should be able to give you suggestions on your presentation and fine tuning your message to resonate with their audience.

   c. This about what clothing and style looks good on you on camera. Your Talk will be on the internet possibly forever, so wear what makes you show well. One rule of TED is no neckties are allowed.

9. Work as directed by the event producers to refine your talk, conduct rehearsals, and plan for the event date.

10. TEDx Talks are presented without notes so practice your talk repeatedly.
    a. To help with your memory retention, practice your speech out loud while multitasking. Say it in the shower, while walking, and other activities so you get comfortable with the process.
11. Closer to the event, participate in on-site or virtual rehearsals.
    a. If you are traveling from outside the region to the event, coordinate with producers, sometimes virtual rehearsals may be an option.
12. Day of event – everything is an adrenaline-fueled blur. Somewhere during that day you got on stage and spoke about something.
    a. You will not remember anything I say here so just manage to enjoy the experience. Also, congratulations!
13. End of the day – you'll likely have an adrenaline crash, crave sugar, and feel giddily exhausted.
    a. I reward my students with a huge basket of comfort food for their trip back home, which gets devoured.
14. Approximately 3 or more months after the event, your video should be available online on TED.com and YouTube.
    a. Reaching this point is a meaningful accomplishment. Humbly accept it as such and continue raising awareness of issues important to you.

Typical TEDx application questions

The following are questions that were required from one TEDx Talk "Call for Speakers" application and are indicative of the questions required in many other applications you'll encounter.

1. Are you on Facebook, Instagram, Tik Tok, Twitter, LinkedIn and if "Yes," how many followers do you have on each platform?
2. Tell us briefly about yourself. (500 characters or less)
3. What would the TEDx talk be about? (400 characters or less)
4. What is the expected time length of your TEDx talk (shorter is better)? [Choices are 5, 6 to 9, 10, 12, 15, or 18 minutes.]
5. What questions do you want to explore in your talk?
6. What is your one Idea Worth Spreading (takeaway message)?
7. Why are you the person to speak on this topic? Please list your job title, your passion, or your credentials as an expert.
8. What will the working title of your talk be? Write a headline that will entice the audience.
9. What value would audience members take from your talk?
10. Please list 3 of your favorite TED or TEDx talks and why you like them.
11. Please list any websites you are affiliated with.
12. Please provide any additional links you'd like us to see.
13. Why do you want to give a TEDx talk?
14. Please tell us something intriguing, remarkable or unexpected about yourself that you have not shared elsewhere on this form?

How to get an Article Published

Understand there are two types of articles that get written: news and editorial. News can be either breaking news or informative pieces that don't have an immediacy to publish. Editorials are opinion pieces where the author is sharing their perspective on a topic. News articles are supposed to be factually accurate and verifiable. Editorials are the author's translation of what they see on an issue. Editorials have traditionally been written by newspaper editors or assigned writers. Guest writers often write Op-Ed articles (which is an old school abbreviation for "Opposite the Editorial page") about their perspectives on a topic.

Many media outlets are open to publishing well-written Op-Eds from a diverse range of writers. The challenge for you, should you want to publish one, is to find the outlet that will find your particular perspective, topic, writing style, and credibility attractive. Learning how to write powerful, credible, interesting Op-Eds is also excellent training for college essays.

I'm focusing primarily on writing Op-Eds here but the same principles apply for writers who want (and know how) to write news stories, which requires adherence to stricter journalistic standards.

Getting published in any media (writing, music, art, research, or other area that interests you) requires a strong level of discipline to send pitches out, get rejected, and send more pitches out. It's not always easy, and that's part of why getting published can be a valuable credential for you.

It's important to let your work speak for itself. I've had situations where a student discusses the importance of their work or the distinctive quality that makes it special, only to find their work doesn't live up to the teaser description. With any piece you want to share, make sure that you are crafting to the best of your abilities. Be a strict critic when it comes to objectively looking at your output, and don't be afraid to make it better if you see where it can be strengthened. Then you can put it out to the world knowing the deliverable is an accurate representation of what you are capable of. If for some reason a member of the public doesn't care for your work, that's fine. Not everybody has to like it, but you can be comforted knowing you've created at a high personal standard of care.

One student I worked with for a short while had a mother who was micromanaging their child's application process. The student wrote an article about a minor charity effort they had created and the mother was determined to get her child's article published. Problem was, the student's effort was insignificant, the charity's impact was overblown, and the article was just plain bad. It was badly written and uninteresting, as if authored by an 8th grader. I did not try to get the article published, even though I could have easily put it up on Medium.com for a link. Instead, the mother got it placed in an online blog and then shared it widely among her circles. She also insisted her child tout it on their resumé with a link. All that was accomplished in that situation was proving to the outside world that her child was not up to par with more accomplished students, the opposite effect of what the mother was intending.

In a different, much more productive situation, after the January 6, 2021 Capitol Riots in Washington, DC, I encouraged one young person I know to write about how many teenagers who were becoming politically aware had only known the recent years of angry political vitriol to be the "normal" standard of political discourse. That writer crafted a thoughtful perspective piece on how they and their friends were feeling after the riots in the Capitol, and how tiring it was to be a young person seeing the "adults" acting so poorly.

[Note: I'm explaining techniques to pitch an Op-Ed piece here, not any particular political stance.]

This is the pitch letter they sent to a shortlist of targeted media outlets:

Sample Pitch Letter

Op-Ed pitch letter example from a young writer:

> February 2, 2021
>
> Dear [Media Outlet] Editorial Team –
>
> I am a documentary photographer, artist, and high school student. [Writer provided some valid credentials on their work in these disciplines.]
>
> I would like to propose the attached and below Op-Ed, "Growing Up During the Trump-Era and How It Messed Me Up," on how the constant violence and anger of the last four years has molded my generation. I am not horrified, outraged or even terrified about last week's domestic terrorist attack on the U.S. Capitol. This has been due to the growing numbness of American teenagers toward the extremism in our country. So, what made the current generation of teenagers so apathetic?
>
> As a 16 year old, I have been attempting to form my identity by observing the world around me. For the last four years, I have been alarmed by the impact of the president of the United States, Donald Trump. Admittedly, the political parties had a lot of trouble communicating opposing viewpoints before Trump, but he serves as a prime model of what has degraded American society to the point where attacking the Capitol on January 6, 2021 became, to many people, an acceptable thing to do.
>
> In contrast to my desensitized attitude, adults who are currently outraged have lived through previous calmer, kinder times so they know what is being lost. People my age; however, only know the vitriol of the past few years. My only practical frame of reference is a president who proudly calls women fat pigs or worse. Growing up in a polarized, angry society during my formative teen years, I didn't have consistent, inspiring leaders to look up to.
>
> If both sides continue their divisive language and actions that blossomed over the last few years, then we as teenagers will be justified in losing all faith in our leaders. What worries me most is that I genuinely do care about our society and civility, but I am no longer shocked by the crimes and violations Americans are inflicting upon each other. And I fear my generation's numbness may become permanent.
>
> I am cc'ing my father, [Father's full name], on this email as an additional contact should you require. Also attached please find a headshot if helpful. Thank you for your consideration.
>
> Sincerely yours,[Writer's full name]

Let's break this effective pitch letter down:

1. The letter in general is written in a mature voice with proper grammar, demonstrating the author's ability as a writer.
2. The author presented their credentials at the start to show that their perspective on the topic is relevant as a thinking young person with a viewpoint.
3. The timeliness of this Op-Ed is spot on. The event being discussed happened only three weeks prior, so media outlets were particularly attuned to publishing on that topic.
4. While that event was being written about by every media outlet in the world, the writer was able to distinguish their article by specifically speaking from the perspective of a young person and contrasting their frame of reference to adults who have experienced multiple presidencies.
5. The proposed headline (which was ultimately changed by the editors) is a bit jarring and unexpected, to further capture the editors' attention.
6. The writer does not confuse opinion with expertise, they know they are speaking only from their vantage point. They are not trying to impose their opinions onto others to follow. They are sharing their perspective and providing what they believe are the underlying influences that shaped their personal opinions.
7. The writer recognizes that the problems have deeper roots, where many individuals and groups have some ownership.
8. They state their concerns for the future if society does not change.
9. They cc'd their father, who is a legal-aged adult, in case the editors had any reservations or concerns communicating with a young writer.
10. The writer made the editor's job a little easier by already attaching a headshot should they need one. It also humanized the writer and may help form a stronger connection once the editors see the writer's face.
11. The email had the article attached as a Microsoft Word document (to assist in editing) and also attached the plain text version at the bottom of the email body, so the editors could continue reading if they were interested in doing so. Any way you can make the screening process easier for editors (or anyone else you are pitching to) the better, so always reduce the number of steps a reviewer has to take to see your work.

The write sent the same message and article to three outlets initially. Within one day, they received this response from one of them, a respected online news site:

> *Thanks for this submission. I'd love to move forward with it -- please let me know if you've placed it elsewhere, though. If not, I can pay you $50 for this and will get any edits I have back to you this week.*

And this response from the second outlet, a major regional newspaper:

Thank you for the submission, but we're going to respectfully decline to run it. We're working through a backlog of op-eds right now and don't have a place for it.

And no response from the third outlet, a national newspaper, which is not uncommon. Because of the volume of submissions they receive, many outlets will only respond if they are interested and not respond for declines.

The writer sent this response back to the editor of the first outlet:

Thank you for your prompt response. It would be a pleasure to work with you. I have not placed this elsewhere, so would welcome your comments and suggestions.

After the first editor agreed to publish the article, they sent back suggested edits seven days later, clarifying points, refining sentences, and even removing 2 paragraphs entirely. The article was reduced from 869 words to 701 words. The writer accepted and made the suggested edits and then sent it back to the editor, who then reviewed it and forwarded the article to their copywriter for final review. The Op-Ed was published online 13 days after initial acceptance, providing the writer with their first real, paid byline.

One of the most important habits to develop – and which many people are weak at doing – is following up. The writer wanted to develop a working relationship with the editor so sent this follow-up message:

Thank you for your thoughtful and valuable edits, I have accepted all of them in the document and clarified other points as you recommended. I really like how you've helped craft it so thank you!

I'd welcome other opportunities to work together, and am committed to raising awareness about both the concerns and hopes of people my age. Are there any upcoming themes that [your outlet] will be featuring where I might consider crafting essay proposals? I'd love to develop a longer-term relationship if I can be supportive of your important work.

And the editor sent back the desired response:

I accept pitches on an ongoing basis, so let me know if you have any ideas for other pieces -- I'd be happy to work together again.

Seeing their article published on the outlet's website was exciting and validating. The $50 payment the writer eventually received was highly satisfying as their first writer's check.

The writer and editor developed a solid working relationship, and the writer (again, they're 16 years old at this time) was invited to become a regular contributor to the outlet, where they would agree to submit one article each month. The editor would typically assign the monthly topics but would also consider topics the writer wanted to suggest. Their goal was to report of current events that readers should be informed of. By the time the writer was applying to colleges, they had published 9 articles for this outlet, in addition to publishing in other distinctive publications. And as of today, they have published 17 articles in that outlet and continued to write monthly articles while they are in college. If they continue on this path, by the time they graduate college they will have an even larger, more impressive portfolio of work that will help distinguish them when they are considering career choices and applying for jobs (ugh, the adulting never ends).

It's fortuitous that the article was picked up so quickly, and I am a firm believer in the maxim "Fortune favors the prepared mind." Looking back to how this journey started, the writer submitted their carefully-crafted article to a small number of media outlets that did not require exclusive first looks on pitches, expecting that most would reject it. Had all three rejected the pitch, the writer had other targets lined up and would have sent out a second wave of pitches, and then a third if necessary. The writer and I knew getting the attention of editors is always challenging, but felt this Op-Ed was strong and worthy for consideration. We were expecting to collect "No's" from the vast majority of editors, and knew that is part of the process. We did believe there was a home for this article somewhere if we were willing to keep searching and pitching well.

Our first and foremost rule for writing an Op-Ed or voicing your opinion publicly in any setting
Punch up, not down.

Back in 1990, before you were born, the comedian George Carlin was interviewed by Larry King regarding a younger, deliberately offensive, misogynistic, racist – yet popular to some crowds – comedian named Andrew Dice Clay who was, at the time, selling out arenas for his crass shows. Decent people might consider his character a pig but that would be insulting to pigs.

Here's the part of the interview that resonated with me (edited for clarity):

George Carlin: *I would defend to the death [Andrew Dice Clay's] right to do everything he does. The thing that I find unusual… his targets are underdogs and comedy traditionally has picked on people in power – people who abuse their power. Women and gays and immigrants are… to my way of thinking underdogs…*

Larry King: *Why does he get away with it do you think?*

George Carlin: *.... I think his core audience are young white males who are threatened by these groups. I think a lot of these guys aren't sure of their manhood because that's a problem when you're going through adolescence you know. Am I really? Am I? Could I be? I hope I'm not one of them. And the women who assert themselves and are competent are a threat to these men and so are immigrants in terms of jobs.... I think that's what is at the core of that experience that takes place in these arenas. There's a certain... sharing of anger and rage and at these targets. And I'm sure Andrew isn't that angry at them, I'm sure he's playing it as a comic.*[8]

Criticize authority all you want. Shine a light on misdeeds, perfidies (good SAT word BTW), deceptions, and malfeasance of governments, corporations, organizations, interest groups, patriarchies, matriarchies, and all others in power. Knock yourself out and have fun doing so.

Do not use your voice or any platform you may have the privilege of using to oppress, belittle, demonize, or otherwise pick on any individual, group or community that is vulnerable or upon which you may hold any advantage over.

Publishing Tips

1. Before you send your article anywhere, have it proofread by someone who is a thoughtful reader and can provide objective edits and feedback. Do not take edits, criticism, or feedback personally, treat it as your professional work. If you are not able to accept comments objectively and without emotion, you probably don't want to be a working writer.

2. Search online for the target media outlet's name along with the keyword "submit" or the phrase "submit an article" to find their submission guidelines. If the outlet does accept outside submissions, the desired page usually is displayed near the top of search results. Some outlets have an online submissions form while others provide an email address for pitches.

3. Recognize that outlets are often understaffed and therefore inundated with pitches. You have to get to the point quickly to get their fleeting attention.

4. Expect to receive many, many more rejections (or no response at all) than the few precious acceptances and plan accordingly. This is where many people stop trying, which is good for you in succeeding. After the first wave of rejection, I find many students get distracted by other

---

[8] Carlin, George, "Charlie Rose Interview - On Comedians Who Pick On The Underdogs," YouTube.com, n.d., https://www.youtube.com/watch?v=F8yV8xUorQ8.

activities and do not continue pitching, so there are unsuccessful due to lack of follow through.

5. If you send your pitch by email, include your article both in the email body as text and a Microsoft Word attachment. Also include a good headshot of yourself.

6. If you are under 18 years old, as a professional courtesy you may want to include your parent or guardian's contact information in the message. If you are under 16 years old, you definitely want to include their contact information.

7. Maintain a list of the pitches you've sent (either in a spreadsheet or using HubSpot as described in *Chapter 7 – Treat your Application Process like a Job*) so you can assess your progress and determine if your approach is working or if you need to make adjustments to get traction with editors. The pitching process is an on-going effort, so your consistency in following up and generating momentum is crucial for eventual success.

Types of Media Outlets to Consider

The range of potential publishers includes national, regional, local, industry-focused, and community-focused media outlets and third-party blogs. There are also open publishing platforms, and – as questionable last resorts – social media or your own website. Understand the different strata of media outlets:

National – These include the New York Times, Wall Street Journal, USA Today, Financial times, and others. The most demanding and difficult to penetrate. It has been done; however, but you've got to have something outstanding. And an inside connection helps. You should strive to write to this standard no matter where you ultimately publish.

Regional – Los Angeles Times, Chicago Tribune, Baltimore Sun, Boston Globe, et al.

Local outlets – I have found that local newspapers and media outlets are often hungry for content and community voices. These local papers may be single-community operations or may sometimes be part of larger media organizations that cover multiple adjacent communities in a region Depending on your article, the larger entities may choose to run your article in your local paper or distribute it across to their other papers as well.

Industry-focused – These media outlets, which may often include online-only sites, can range anywhere from stock picking to videogame development to antique car restorers to knitting.

Community-focused – These outlets may resonate with specific communities, ranging from women's empowerment to LGBT+ to cultural and other communities.

Third-party blogs – The editorial quality of independent blogs varies wildly; however, getting published on a respectable blog has its merit. Contacting the site owner is easier than any of the above and it would give you an independent platform to link to. Be conscientious of whom you target because you want to ensure the tone, perspective, and quality of their content is in line with yours.

A list of prospective major media outlets with links to their submission guidelines is included in the Appendix.

NOTE FOR ASPIRING NEWS WRITERS: I have found local, industry-focused, and community-focused outlets to be the most open to publishing guest features for relevant news stories, and more likely for general news than for time-sensitive breaking news reports. If the outlet's website does not specify how or where to pitch, you may have to email the News Editor with your proposal. You should have your article already written (conforming to Associated Press reporting standards) and include it in your email.

My students and I target prospective publications based on the topic, tone, and target audience of the article being pitched. The scope of your article will determine the appropriate targets. Put together a wish list of outlets you want to pitch and methodically send out pitches. Some outlets require you to only pitch them (that is, no simultaneous pitching while they are considering you) but others are okay knowing you're pitching multiple outlets at the same time. To help determine where you article might be best placed, ask yourself these questions:

Is the issue you are writing about something of neighborhood, statewide, national, or international interest?

Who is the audience? Everyone or specific people who tend to fall in certain demographics?

What publications resonate with your article's target audience?

Open platforms for publishing

A handful of respectable outlets exist that allow most anybody to publish their writing, and these sites can be a valid way to launch your publishing efforts, including the ability to publish multiple articles or series which can reinforce evidence of your subject matter knowledge. The open sites I recommend considering include Medium.com, LinkedIn.com, and Boredpanda.com to help you build a portfolio of writing as you continue to pursue curated publishing.

Medium.com allows you to publish articles on any topic and, if enough people read your articles, supposedly make a little money as well. Don't do Medium for the money as there's not much of it for most people. Medium does; however, provide a quality website you can point to. Medium also allows you to create your own magazine on their platform, which gives you opportunity to be more creative in potentially building a wider following, provided you continue to generate articles on your topic or invite other writers to contribute articles to your online magazine.

LinkedIn.com allows you to write and publish articles, which get shared with your network. Because LinkedIn is primarily focused on working professionals the articles are written accordingly, but there's no rule that says they must strictly be business-focused articles. Whatever your topic, if you can reasonably position it to be relevant to this audience, LinkedIn could be a suitable platform. Do some research on the types of articles that have been written on your area and see if you can add to that body of knowledge.

Boredpanda.com is a visually-strong site with articles that usually contain a lot of images in the storytelling. It is well-suited for photo essays, interesting lists or collections with images.

As a comparison, searching for the keyword "guitar" on all three sites brought up these types of articles:

Medium.com: "I needed a guitar teacher, so I turned my Alexa into one" and "Chord Assist: Building an accessible smart guitar for the blind, deaf, and mute"

LinkedIn.com: "Charvel/Jackson Early History 1974-1980" [that's an electric guitar brand]

Boredpanda.com: "I Crafted My Own Pinocchio Diorama Inside a Guitar (10 Pics)" and "I Turn Broken Skateboards Into Electric Guitars"

DIY Publishing

If all else fails, you can post to social media, your own website, or your blog. The value and impact of your work will be weighed accordingly.

Resources for better writing

The OpEd Project

www.theopedproject.org

The OpEd Project promotes knowledge and connections across color, creed, class, age, ability, gender, orientation, and beyond. Through their programs they elevate the ideas and knowledge of underrepresented expert voices, including women. They offer a 2-day online workshop "Write to Change the World" where they teach how to write with credibility; the patterns and elements of persuasion; the difference between being "right" and being effective; how to preach beyond the choir; and how to think bigger about what you know to have more impact. The workshop costs about $375 if you register early (about 2 months in advance) and $480 regularly. They offer need-based scholarship up to 30 percent of the program cost to those who qualify.

How to Publish a Book Fast

Publishing a book is a meaningful way to demonstrate that you have the ability to see major projects through to completion as well as showcase your subject matter knowledge. Publishing a book is likely a bucket list goal to many people (who will probably never achieve it) and can be a source of pride for the author who gets the job done. There are few teenagers – a miniscule number even – who have gone through the process of taking an idea in their head to words on the page to editing (repeatedly) to formatting to publishing and getting a book onto the printed page, neatly bound with beautiful cover art.

Fortunately, that can be you. There is traditional publishing, which typically requires getting picked up by a literary agent who then would seek to sell your book to a publisher. At its fastest rate, this process takes at least a couple of years from start to finish. It's great for those authors who can accomplish that, but realistically that is not you today.

Amazon's Kindle Direct Publishing ("KDP") has become a respectable (and sometimes profitable) option for authors to self-publish in every subject and every written fiction and non-fiction format. Whatever topic you're considering publishing likely has been done in some way already, but you can make yours distinctive by lending your voice and perspective to your book.

You have tremendous freedom on what you can publish, here are some suggestions but the options are near limitless based on your interests and efforts:

Non-fiction	**Fiction**

- Art and photography
- Biography
- Business and money
- Companion guides to school courses you have already taken
- Cooking
- Crafts, hobbies
- Education and teaching
- Families and relationships
- Health and fitness
- History
- Humor and entertainment
- Instruction manuals, "How to" books
- Law and criminology
- Low-content books (e.g., blank journals)
- Memoir and autobiography
- Motivational and inspirational
- Politics and political science
- Research reports
- Religion and spirituality
- Reviews (movie, book, art, music or other reviews)
- Self-help, personal development
- Travel
	- Illustrated books, graphic novels
	- Novels of all type
	   - Fantasy
	   - Science fiction
	   - Dystopian (you are a teenager, after all)
	   - Adventure
	   - Romance
	   - Mystery
	   - Horror
	   - Thriller
	   - LGBTQ+
	   - Historical fiction
	   - Young adult
	   - Children's fiction
	- Poetry

In terms of the speed to complete and emotional pain suffered in completing a manuscript, the following genres – in my opinion – are listed in least-painful to most-painful order.

Low-content books – Low-content books include items such as blank journals or password keeper books where the book owner fills in the content. Do this only if you have a really interesting, new idea that meets a niche need to show you gave it a lot of thought and aren't just printing blank books. If you want your name attached to a low-content book, it should be for a highly-specific topic or purpose that ties into your interests and is an improvement on existing products, such as "The Scuba Diver's Log, Data Record, and Dive Journal for Southern Hemisphere Waters" or "The Daily Meditation, Gratitude, Reflection, and Aspiration Journal for [fill in a specific demographic]." Low content books are not considered serious writing since there is little writing in them.

Crafts / Hobbies – These books might include compendiums, unofficial guides, directories, price guides, or other reference lists. Discussing your topic in a thorough, book-length manner is important. This also might be the most enjoyable type of writing a person can do if they like the topic.

Instruction / How To books – Here you are taking information that already exists somewhere and reconstituting it for public consumption. Using ChatGPT or other AI-generated paraphrasing tools can make this job dramatically easier. When you write an instruction or How To book, you become a somewhat de facto expert on your topic, whether that be cybersecurity or needlepoint or pet care.

Companion guides for school courses – This category is similar to Instruction / How To books, although it will require explanation of possibly theoretical or otherwise hard-to-explain concepts. Companion guides to school courses you have already taken may be one area where you've done (or experienced) most of the work already. Use your class notes. Don't plagiarize from your textbooks.

Children's fiction and illustrated books – If you wanted to crank something out quickly, not caring about the book's quality or merit, you can consider a children's book. That being said, if you're going to do a half-assed job it's not worth starting in the first place. And it's not something you'd want to your name associated with. To create a good children's book that is not pandering and may have longevity requires a lot of thinking, creativity, and skill.

Self-help / Inspirational – Do as I say, not as I do. There's a lot of noise in this category so if you're going to venture here, do try your best to write something that conveys real wisdom to the reader, not just platitudes or regurgitated motivational speaking.

Art and Photography – It's easy to fill pages with photos, captions, and graphics. The challenge is making it something worth reading and viewing. If your images resonate with viewers, that's a good feeling.

Poetry – I don't understand good poetry from lesser forms, but I do know people who can appreciate the difference. They will recognize those books filled with fluff and quickly discard them, and appreciate books with quality writing.

Research / History – The pain level you'll experience depends on whether you are aggregating and repackaging existing research (perhaps to make it more easily understood) or are you generating original research.

Fiction – This type of prose requires your full creativity and skill so of course you want it to be perfect. It's hard not to take criticism personally regarding your fiction writing.

Autobiographical – Even more painful than fiction writing, as you'll likely feel criticism even more sharply. Especially during holiday family gatherings after publication.

Self-published books on Amazon have a page count requirement as low as 24 pages so you don't have to feel pressure to create a monumental volume, just the best one you are capable of creating. You can create both paperback and hardcover versions of your book. You can also publish either a companion eBook to your print book or you may decide to just publish an eBook without print versions. The low page count was conducive for one person to publish their illustrated children's book in both paperback and hardcover.

I helped one of my students self-publish a book they had written, which was a guide and instruction manual for certain technical skills. For that client, writing a manual was a good choice for a few reasons:

- Writing a guide or instruction manual is a lot like writing an extensive book report. The goal is to write clearly and concisely, there may not be need for extensive prose;

- They were able to footnote extensive sources for the different procedures and topics discussed, which lent credibility to the contents;

- Because they were writing on a specific topic rather than something creative or autobiographical, their personal angst and creative struggle were dramatically diminished (they didn't take edits or criticisms personally); and

- Because it was an informational guide, it did not have to be grippingly interesting either, instead it had to get the facts out efficiently.

That particular manual included extensive screenshots of the work being discussed, which helped add to the heft while also making a technical topic more digestible. A high page count is not a requirement. Anything you write (book-length or otherwise) should have the necessary number of words to convey what you intend, not more words or less words than needed.

The Kindle Direct Publishing site has exhaustive instructions to get your book published so it's not additive to repeat them here. Below are production and marketing tips to consider that will make your process more efficient, based on my personal experience:

Production Tips

I have used these tips to move through the manuscript setup process efficiently and will hopefully save you many days' time by not having to figure them out yourself:

1. Microsoft Word is the best word processor to format your document, including automated Table of Contents, bibliography, and index as needed.

2. For nonfiction, use Zotero (www.zotero.com) for manage your citations, as it has a Word add-in to help manage your footnotes.

3. To create attractive Table of Contents for books with headings and subheadings (such as in instructional books), learn to use the Styles feature in Word, which creates different level headings and styles in

your book as needed. Not using Styles will result in spending a lot of time fixing page-by-page formatting later.

4. For printed books, KDP requires you to upload a PDF file but, for ebooks, KDP requires you upload a Word document, so plan accordingly.

5. You can create a front and back cover using KDP's online tools, or create your own in Adobe PhotoShop or similar program. If you are creating your own cover, the spine width and any color bleed edges need to be accurate based on book dimensions and page count, so use KDP's "Print Cover Calculator and Templates" feature (https://kdp.amazon.com/en_US/cover-calculator) to get the exact size requirements for the cover you'll produce. Trying to do this through trial and error is extremely time consuming.

6. Most people are not equipped to create a high quality, interesting book cover. If you want to find someone with experience, consider posting a project request on Fiverr.com where you can hire a freelancer to design a cover for you at a moderate price. Alternatively, you can try using AI-generated artwork from sites such as DALL-E 2 (https://openai.com/dall-e-2/).

7. Once you are ready to upload your files, the rendering and review process to preview your book is slow, taking many minutes so expect to be patient. As you make adjustments to your book, you'll have to bear with the slow re-rendering.

Marketing Tips

One of the positive benefits of KDP is you get to determine the price of your book, which then determines the net royalty you could receive, You might even make a few dollars on this, which is satisfying and a bit validating (even if only your family bought it). Since you put your best efforts into producing a quality product you understandably want the widest audience possible. Here are some procedures that can help promote your book:

1. Now that you've written and published your book, you should understand that – if you want to actually make money off your book – writing the book is about 25 percent of the work, marketing it is the other 75 percent.

2. Create a free Authors Page on Amazon where you can include your bio and credentials.

3. Reviews are important, reviews from verified purchasers are even better. Ask friends and family to read and leave HONEST reviews on Amazon. I stress honest because fake, overly glowing reviews are easy to spot and detract from credibility.

4. Create a full PDF of your book (including covers and a page linking to your Amazon listing) and label it **REVIEW COPY**. Think creatively of

whom you might be able to send it to for possible review including bloggers in your space, industry experts (aim high, right?), and writers at relevant websites. You may consider sending those potential reviewers a polite, well-written email asking if they'd be interested in receiving a digital copy of your book either for potential review or just as a reference for their use (do not send the PDF in this email, you are just asking for interest). If they respond positively, then send the PDF and ask them to apprise you if they do review the book. Also accept and feedback or critique they may be willing to provide.

5. Create a scaled down PDF of your book and label it **PREVIEW COPY** (with covers and Amazon link). This is a teaser copy, with a handful of interesting chapters that would encourage the reader to purchase your entire book. Consider if there are any community or niche interest groups on LinkedIn, Facebook or elsewhere where you can post the publication of your new book and offer to share a free preview copy should anyone be interested in taking a look. You can also ask them to consider leaving an Amazon review should the choose. You're not trying to push hard here (that's tacky), instead you are willing to share information with the broader public on your topic.

6. Consider setting up a small marketing budget on Amazon to tie your book to the top sellers in your category. Using KDP marketing, you can create sponsored placement when users search for specific titles. For a few different books, I've created marketing campaigns linked to the top 5 selling titles in their categories with budgets of a few dollars per day. It was a good learning experience to understand the dynamics of paid marketing.

Regardless if you sell or not, if you did create a work that you believe represents the quality you are capable of achieving, then by all means be proud of your accomplishment and present this worthy credential in your college applications.

And in the far back of your mind, consider what your next book might be about. One book is impressive, two or more over time are even more so for your longer-term growth and aspirations.

How to Create an Online Course

The student can become the master. Switching hats from tutee to tutor is a milestone for anyone. Being able to teach a subject implies that you've reached a point where you know what you're talking about. One concrete way to demonstrate this knowledge is by creating an online course where you explain concepts clearly to an audience. Creating a quality course on any subject you enjoy is a distinctive way to demonstrate subject matter knowledge, because teaching well requires some level of mastery. It also demonstrates that you care to share information with others.

I have found Udemy.com to be the most effective platform for individuals to create online courses. Platforms such as Coursera.com only host courses offered by schools. Udemy's site has extensive instructions on the steps needed to create your course.

You should determine if you prefer being onscreen to teach or narrating from offscreen to slides, images and video. Both are acceptable options.

Planning an informative course requires a thoughtful planning process, including:

1. Define your course topic and the type of students you want to target;
2. Create learning objectives;
3. Outline your course;
4. Plan practice activities and assessments;
5. Produce content;
6. Publish your course;
7. Market your course;
8. Engage with students; and
9. Iterate on content

More specifically, consider these steps:
1. Define your course topic and the type of students you want to target
    a. This research can help you determine if there is a need for the course before investing time and energy into creating it. You can see on Udemy how popular your topic is by the number of existing courses that exist. Can you present the information in a new way or from your distinct perspective?
    b. Arguably, if you market is oversaturated with similar courses you could still create a course for the purposes of listing it in

your application, but that is not a good use of your precious time. Strive to become an original voice.

2. Create learning objectives
    a. Consider what your target students will gain from taking your course by studying the target audience you've identified. Before creating any content, set tangible learning objectives that define the information, skillsets, and attitudes students should obtain after completing your course. This approach helps to focus on essential topics as well as guaranteeing that all goals are met effectively.

3. Outline your course
    a. The course outline serves as the cornerstone of your class. You will have to decide how comprehensive or focused your course will be to best educate your audience.

4. Plan practice activities and assessments
    a. As you plan and construct your content to help students reach their educational goals, don't forget to add practical exercises and tests like quizzes, drills, and labs that enable them to apply what they learn while gauging their understanding of the material.

5. Produce content
    a. Now that you have the framework of your course, it's time to plan for filming your lectures. Many instructors find scripting each lecture (or writing bullet point notes) is helping in decreasing their recording length and improving their delivery. This step includes producing videos, articles, resources, exercises, and assessments that will be shared during the entire course progress.

6. Publish your course
    a. Upload your course content on Udemy and write the course landing page copy and automatic messages. Submitted courses are reviewed by Udemy's Trust & Safety team to ensure the course meets requirements before it's published on Udemy.

7. Market your course
    a. Generate enthusiasm for your course by distributing discounts to your network if it can help build momentum. Acquire feedback about what you've developed. Udemy offers different marketing initiatives to help you take advantage of their wide-reaching promotions.

8. Engage with students

- a. After you release your course, you have the opportunity to interact with students. You can address inquiries and provide useful feedback on assignments for optimum engagement.
9. Iterate on content
    - a. To stay ahead of the curve, it is essential to renew your course content regularly. Refresh any courses immediately when an industry shift occurs; students offer feedback; or you have new dynamic material to contribute.

Submit your Research Paper to Conferences

There's been a lot of high quality research on complex topics and disciplines that's been conducted by high school students. The problem is, most of the world doesn't know it exists. What's worse, even the practitioners in those disciplines don't know it exists because so much student research never sees a life beyond the student's laptop.

If you have a research paper that is solid enough to socialize with knowledgeable peers, consider taking the bold step of submitting your research to industry conferences for presentation or publication. Many conferences issue Call for Papers ("CFPs") well in advance of the event date where practitioners can share their new research to others in their field. To be accepted into a conference, your paper would be peer reviewed just like a scientific publication would require, but possibly at a faster and incrementally less-demanding standard. That is not to suggest you submit sloppy work, you must hold yourself to the same demanding standards other researchers do. Going through the highly-educational process of submitting your paper and presenting at a conference can be a meaningful step toward publication in a peer-reviewed journal.

Conferences serve as invaluable outlets for researchers to engage in and share their work. I recognize that presenting at an industry conference is probably the last thing any high school student feels qualified to do, and that's fine for most everyone. This isn't a mandatory coming-of-age ritual or anything, but if you want to do something meaningfully unexpected, this certainly qualifies. It demonstrates without question your interest in your discipline and desire to be at the forefront of discovery. This is also the type of accomplishment where your young age makes it ridiculously notable.

Many conferences provide written guidelines, formats, and instructions on how to prepare your Call for Papers submission, which can help make the process less daunting. It is also good for you to become familiar with the standards your field requires so you can navigate similar opportunities more easily over time.

To submit your paper to a conference, you need an abstract that concisely explains why the topic is compelling, what problem it attempts to solve, and how others will benefit from this information. When you're ready to submit your paper for a conference, make sure that it follows the style and structure of published papers in your field of study, as well as any specific requirements listed in the call for papers. Your presentation needs to be academically sound while also relevant to the particular conference.

Be aware that conference organizers often require selected presenters to pay for their admission ticket, just like the attendees have to pay so budget accordingly.

Listed below are online directories of upcoming conferences where you can find opportunities. I recommend applying to as many as logistically possible, as you don't know where you may be accepted. There will be events that are several months out, possibly into the following year. Take a long-term view of the process and apply where it makes sense, even if the event is well past your college application date. Should you be accepted to a conference, being able to state in your college applications that you will be presenting your research at an upcoming conference is just as impressive as having already done so. And regardless of the college application process, if you are interested in your topic you hopefully should want to continue engaging in research, no matter where you are going to school.

If and when your paper gets selected for a conference, you will be expected to give a brief presentation on your research. Put together an engaging yet concise slideshow presentation based on your paper, then be ready to answer any questions from the audience.

You may be allowed the opportunity to present a poster display at the conference as well. Strive for visuals that are easy to comprehend and incorporate them into your design for maximum appeal. Make sure the poster looks like something you'd see on a billboard – not just a copy of your paper printed out and taped up on cardboard. You should search online for examples of effective presentation slideshows and poster displays in your field.

Directories of industry conferences

CFP List

https://www.cfplist.com/

This an academic Call for Papers database where users can search for publication opportunities, including in the following search categories:

1. American History
2. British History
3. Comparative
4. Digital Humanities
5. Engineering
6. French
7. Gender & Sexuality
8. Genre & Form
    a. Adventure & Travel Writing
    b. Children's Literature
    c. Comics & Graphic Novels
    d. Drama
    e. Narratology
    f. Poetry
9. German
10. Graduate Conference
11. Interdisciplinary
    a. Aesthetics
    b. Anthropology/Sociology
    c. Classical Studies
    d. Cultural Studies

e. Environmental Studies
   f. Film, TV, & Media
   g. Food Studies
   h. History
   i. Philosophy
   j. Popular Culture
12. Linguistics
13. Literary Theory
14. Miscellaneous
15. Pedagogy
16. Rhetoric & Composition
17. Science
18. Women's Studies
19. World Literatures

200+ Best Conferences to Attend

https://www.aventri.com/strategy/top-conferences-to-attend-this-year

This is a comprehensive list of in-person, virtual and hybrid conferences.

WikiCFP

http://www.wikicfp.com/cfp/

This is a semantic wiki for Calls For Papers in science and technology fields. According to the site, there are more than 100,000 CFPs on WikiCFP and over 100,000 researchers use WikiCFP each month.

Conal Conference Alerts

https://conferencealerts.com/

This an online calendar for academic and professional events worldwide.

How to Exhibit your Art

Finding opportunities to exhibit your artwork is important in the development of intentional or serious artists. The logistics involved in exhibiting, such as preparing, framing, packing, delivery, hanging, displaying, and then taking down your piece or exhibit is valuable experience to accumulate. Learning to write compelling artist statements (and using words like "praxis" correctly) as well as technically accurate descriptions of your art pieces are also important skills to develop for artists.

If you are interested in getting your artwork exhibited, there are a number of channels you can consider including (in order of increasing difficulty):

- Self-curated shows and pop-up exhibits,
- Non-curated group shows,
- Online galleries,
- Curated group shows / competitions,
- Curated member-only shows / competitions,
- Gallery exhibits, and
- Museum exhibits

Exhibition Channels

Here's a rundown of the different channels to consider for exhibition opportunities. Links are included to provide a better feel for what is expected from the representative venue or show. The span of opportunities for artists is vast, these examples are by no way representative of all the opportunities you can consider but are helpful reference.

Self-curated shows and pop-up exhibits

These are likely self-funded exhibits so be prepared to cover the costs. Arguably you can exhibit your art anywhere you are able. I don't recommend pulling a Banksy and hanging your work in the Tate (it would be derivative by now); however, you may consider seeking opportunities where you can put up your own exhibit. You can, of course, assemble a group show if more suitable. I've seen opportunities of this nature in a wide range of not-for-profit venues and common areas such as hospital waiting rooms. You might be able to keep an installation in place for meaningful periods of time depending on the venue's needs.

For temporary pop-up exhibits, consider if there are events being organized by third parties where you could offer to set up an exhibit that complements their event and enhances the audience experience. If you are flexible in your thinking and willing to write a good email pitch, you may find that event planners working with limited budgets would welcome suitable exhibitors. [Granted, to determine if your art can be additive to someone else's theme, you first have to know what your own theme is. If you've conducted that level of self-reflection, Congratulations. If you haven't and aren't sure how to do so, consider listening to some of the Praxis Center courses noted below or Google how to do so.]

For my documentary photography, I have had pop-up exhibits at several events and conferences sponsored by not-for-profits or universities. Because I keep apprised of activity related to my field of interest through newsletters and general paying attention, I have a consistent information flow of upcoming events. I have independently contacted organizers to share my work and offer to support their event by decorating their space with my photo portraits. Because I can drive myself, and I have some budget to spend on exhibit materials such as easels and signage, I create a visually-impactful exhibit that can be transported wherever I please. I also wrote some nicely-worded emails to suppliers who were willing to print and frame my work at steep discounts because they were supportive of the exhibit's purpose. All of this was a learning experience for me and will be for you should you want to do so. After the event I asked the organizers for a letter of reference, which I could include in future exhibit proposals. I view these types of exhibits as grassroots efforts. I am highly resourceful in gathering the materials and supplies needed to put on a visually-stunning show as economically as possible. To the outside viewer, it appears professionally and credibly assembled, and only I know that I used a lot of duct tape and zip ties behind the scenes to make it all come together.

Non-curated group shows

These are shows where the general public is invited and encouraged to submit their artwork for display, and all pieces are accepted by the show organizer.

For example, the not-for-profit visual arts center Artworks Trenton, which promotes artistic diversity and appreciation located in Trenton, NJ, organizes their annual Art All Night event. Any artist of any age, skill level or medium is invited to submit one piece of artwork for this 24-hour show. (www.artallnighttrenton.org)

New York City's Museum of Modern Art ("MOMA") organized a public show back in 2002 called Life of the City, which I participated in. In conjunction with an exhibit of photographs from the museum's collection, the museum organized a display of photographs contributed by New Yorkers and visitors that express their relationships to the city. While technically my photograph was exhibited by MOMA, I'm careful not to overstate the parameters in which it was displayed, Nevertheless, inwardly it was a nice feeling knowing I had something briefly hanging on the walls of MOMA, a museum I am in awe of. (www.moma.org/calendar/exhibitions/156)

Publications or online galleries

There are numerous outlets where you may be able to have your piece or pieces shared, including blogs, articles, or third-party websites. The onus is on you to initiate the outreach and explore opportunities to share your work.

Chaffey College's Wignall Museum in California, for example, issued an open call for artists to consider how hip hop has influenced the world for an online virtual project, open to all media and practices that can be shared online using photographic, video, or other digital file formats. (www.chaffey.edu/wignall/hip-hop-summit.php)

Curated group shows

These shows invite all artists to submit their works for consideration, usually requiring an entry fee. Awards are issued, sometimes with a monetary prize.

The public not-for-profit Cultural Center of Cape Cod, for example, issued a Call to amateurs and professionals worldwide, with all styles and aesthetics considered. Their upcoming show was focused on motion and movement, so were seeking hangings, sculptures, mobiles, and paintings to create a moving, 3-D experience. (www.cultural-center.org)

Curated member-only shows

These curated shows are open to members of an organization or society, so the number of applicants is typically smaller than a public show but can still be sizeable and highly competitive. Many museums may organize Member Shows.

For the last 80 years, Audubon Artists has held an annual members exhibition, awarding $20,000 in cash and merchandise awards in 2022. They also have an online bi-monthly showcase which features randomly-selected members who have submitted requests, sharing works on their website and social media. (www.audubonartisis.org)

Gallery exhibits

For our purposes, galleries include any venue where your art may be exhibited with the possibility of being sold. That can include formal gallery spaces as well as your local coffee shop or restaurant willing to hang your pieces on their wall. Many galleries hold open calls and are listed in the directory websites listed below. For local venues such as coffee shops and other establishments (you should be open-minded when brainstorming potential locations) you'll need to be proactive in your outreach and proposal of what you would like to display, for how long, and within what parameters so you work can be additive to the venue's operations and mission.

Museum exhibits

Museums may organize competitions open to the general public. Some museums organize annual shows specifically for young artists (i.e., YOU) and sometimes have geographic or other requirements for participants. A sample list of museums that organize annual Youth shows include:

- Alexandria Museum of Art – Alexandria, LA

- Bruce Museum – Greenwich, CT
- Bullock Museum – Austin, TX
- Heard Museum Guild, American Indian Youth Art Show + Sale – Phoenix, AZ
- Museum of Photographic Arts – San Diego, CA
- Red River Valley Museum – Vernon, TX
- Rockford Art Museum – Rockford, IL
- San Diego Museum of Art biennial – San Diego, CA
- Young at Art Museum fashion show – Plantation, FL
- And many others you can search for

Now, I want you to understand I listed the above Youth shows to make you feel better about the possibility of being selected to exhibit in a museum. If your work is solid it is entirely possible to be accepted into Youth shows. For the general Youth population these opportunities are great and have merit. For your purposes of distinguishing yourself and letting your work speak for itself; however, you should be willing to be bolder. You should seriously consider submitting your strongest pieces to Calls for Entries for the broader population (those targeting aspiring and working adult artists) to push your craft further and raise the standards to which you create.

Sometimes a Call for Entry may require an applicant to be 18 years old or older. In those circumstances, if it's something you really want to enter, I'm willing to let you lie about your age. It's not like you're committing a federal crime. If you do win some prize; however, you should 'fess up and decline the acceptance so an eligible artist can receive it. It's the noble thing to do and also would give you a really good story to share at parties (and possibly in a college essay too). High quality problem if it ever occurs.

Directories of Open Call Opportunities

Here are some resources that can help you gain perspective and insight into finding available opportunities.

Art Call

www.artcall.org

Art Call is a website that maintains a current list of many open calls for both online and physical art shows in the U.S. and Canada. Listings include Competitions, Exhibitions, Fairs and Festivals, Residencies, Workshops, Grants and Fellowships, and Proposals for Public Art. Search results can be filtered by state. The event organizers pay a fee to post their Call for Entry so it does not include every possible Call; however, it is extensive and a good resource to keep abreast of opportunities.

Art Connect

www.artconnect.com

Art Connect is a website that lets you search for opportunities, where you can narrow your search for Open Calls, Awards and Prizes, Grants and Stipends, Collaborations, Residencies, Commissions, Education, and Jobs. You can specify the objective you are seeking, including Exhibition, Publication, Cash Prize, Accommodation, Production, and Travel. You can also select Calls that are free or require a fee to submit your application.

Call For Entry

www.callforentry.org

Call For Entry is another site offering search categories for Youth, Member, Alumni, and Performing Arts in addition to the general categories on the above sites.

Learn about the Business of Art

This below is an insightful resource for learning how to navigate the sometimes-confusing and opaque art world.

Praxis Center for Aesthetic Studies

www.praxiscenterforaestheticstudies.com

One valuable and informative resource I've used for real-world insight into the art industry, and what aspiring artists can use for advancing their praxis (see what I did there) is getting a monthly subscription to the Praxis Center for Aesthetic Studies. This is Netflix for art insight, filled with an abundance of instructional videos that get to the point quickly. Monthly fees run between $40 and $60 and, if you are determined, you can binge watch a huge number of insightful videos in a month and then cancel your subscription if budget is an issue. What originally attracted me to this site was listening to the founder, a working artist named Brainard Carey, explain how he was selected for the Whitney Museum of Art's Biennial Exhibit, a highly influential and prestigious survey of American art.

Some of the many topics include: Art world Etiquette; Communicating with Curators; The Importance of Not-for-profit Exhibitions; Getting into Art Galleries; Instagram for Artists; How to Write your Biography; and others. This level of insight is intended for aspiring working artists and would be extremely powerful knowledge in the hands (or head) of a young emerging artist who is bold enough to act on it.

How to get Quoted in the Media

Beyond writing articles for publication, you may want to contribute to other writer's articles as an information source. There are several areas where teenagers possess inherent subject matter expertise that older people lack. In particular, teenagers often are much faster, more adept, more knowledgeable, and more willing to adopt or adapt to:

- New devices and gadgets;
- New online platforms (such as AI-powered apps);
- New social media communities;
- New vocabulary;
- New fashion trends;
- New influences and influencers; and
- Teenage experiences of every type

Additionally, since you've been working on developing your specific subject matter knowledge, you hopefully are increasingly capable of opining on that topic as well.

When writing news articles, journalists often desire to include quotes, perspectives, or information provided by subject matter experts to lend credibility to their articles. To find those subject matter experts, journalists may put out information requests through different websites, including:

Helpareporter.com (commonly known as HARO)

Qwoted.com

Helpareporter.com

HARO has numerous daily requests (known as "queries") from journalists seeking sources. There is a free version as well as a Standard $19 monthly plan. HARO notes that media outlets that use their platform include Reuters, New York Times, Chicago Tribune, ABC, Wall Street Journal, and other major outlets. There are also many other news and industry outlets posting queries daily.

In HARO, you register yourself as a Source (not a Reporter) and provide basic information. They send out a 3-times-a-day email listing the new Reporter queries they've received. They offer a catch-all Master list of all new queries (which can be lengthy to get through), or you can opt to receive a subset list of queries in these categories: High Tech, General, Travel, Business and Finance, Lifestyle and Fitness, Giftbag, and UK.

The Giftbag category is organizations asking for product donations to put into event-related giftbags, which can provide the donor some bragging rights or marketing collateral to use. If you happen to have a new consumer product you are marketing, this may be something to pay attention to. If you have an actual service to offer, many requestors will take coupons or gift certificates as well.

With 3 emails a day, HARO can become voluminous in your inbox and distracting for your time. Their Standard $19 plan allows you to create 1 filtered email that matches your keyword preferences (which I find efficient because my custom alert is for my specific niche). The Standard plan allows you to create a Profile that reporters can view, where you provide an "About Me" description as well as summaries of your expertise, publications, media experience, memberships, and education. The profile has fields for your website, blog, Twitter, Facebook, and LinkedIn should you choose to provide them. You can also use the keyword search to sift through their database of current query opportunities.

The posted queries typically include the requesting reporter's name and publication they are writing for, so you can determine if there's a fit with your branding goals. Some reporters choose to be anonymous, but that should not necessarily discourage you from responding. If a reporter is interested in using your quote, they should be contacting you to confirm your information prior to publication.

Your response is called a Pitch, where you would present a brief summary of your credentials (even if they're included in your Profile) and then cleanly and concisely answer their specific questions with credible, even citable, information. You also want to include a credit line, such as "[Your full name] is a student at [High school name] in [City, State]" or, if possible, something more creative. You also should include a website link to either your personal website or public-facing social media handle (we discuss your social media presence in *Chapter 13 – Develop Your Personal Brand*). You should also have a proper headshot available if the reporter requests one for inclusion in the article.

For illustrative purposes, here are two queries that were found when searching for the phrase "Gen Z." The have been edited slightly to anonymize the reporters and publications.

This first one is a good query to pitch to demonstrate subject matter knowledge.

Publication: a cybersecurity industry news and information website

Query: Studies have shown that despite being seen as more tech-savvy than other generations, Gen Z are actually less cyber-aware and cyber-secure than other generations. I'm seeking contributors who can help answer these questions: Why do you think Gen Z is less cyber secure, despite growing up with more access to technology than other generations? - How can companies try and combat this? Relevant studies/case/studies or examples that you can share, if available, are welcome.

Requirements: I'm looking for comments from people who have cyber security positions but DO NOT work for cyber security companies. Answers to each question should be 300 words MAX.

A high schooler might fall short on the above stated requirements, but bear in mind that the reporter may have not thought of asking high schooler for their opinion so you responding could be invigorating, unexpected, and welcome to the reporter if they are seeking to write a well-rounded article:

This next one is a perfectly good query for someone else but would be harmful to you developing a well-regarded brand that would resonate positively with admissions boards, so you would avoid this at all costs:

Publication: a general news website with a heavy focus on celebrity gossip.

Query: I'm working on a feature about the luxury goods market which is being propped up by Millennials/Generation Z. I'm interested in hearing from people who live at home with their parents and use their money to invest in designer bags and other goods.

Requirements: You must be willing to be named and have your picture appear.

Remember, the goal here is to develop and advance your personal branding image in an impressive, credible manner where you can be recognized for your skills and talents. The first query above can help you in that regard, the second query would not.

Qwoted.com

Qwoted's free plan allows you to respond to 3 queries per month. They send daily emails out and reading them is more time consuming that HARO's email because Qwoted free membership sends out their catch-all list of ever new query to subscribers. Their paid plan is $99 per month, which is probably now worthwhile for your purposes. Qwoted notes that their site is used by the Associated Press, Reuters, New York Times, Forbes, Huffington Post, and many other respected names. Similar to HARO, there are many industry or smaller outlets posting queries daily.

It takes consistent effort to stay abreast of reporter queries, even with these two aggregator sites and their daily emails. There is strong benefit from being quoted in respectable publications if the opportunity arises, so this is a helpful strategy to have in your arsenal of resources.

How to Create your Portfolio Website

At this stage in your life, there's low value in creating a website that showcases you, your personality, and how special you are. There can be high value; however, in creating a website that shares your portfolio of work, which hopefully informs, enlightens, and even inspires the viewer. A portfolio website is about your work, not so much about you, and – designed properly – will permit your work to speak for itself so viewers can determine if they find your skills valid and credible.

One of the best things about creating a portfolio website as compared to a personality website is a portfolio website doesn't care what you look like, or what clothes you wear, or if you have style, six-pack abs, or straight teeth. Andy Warhol didn't become the Andy Warhol we envision until after he was famous.

Look at other people you admire in your field and see if their personal websites have elements you would want to emulate. It's perfectly acceptable to mimic existing good design. Just make sure to personalize it to best represent you.

Also take a look at websites built by other high schoolers and see if there are elements you do not like and determine why. Are there elements that make the overall site too casual, not tight, or just amateurish? Don't do those same things.

A portfolio website does not have to be extensive. In fact, it's better to keep your mediocre work off of it rather than feel you must have a lengthy gallery of examples to show. Keep it simple, mostly because it takes time to build a website and you can get mired in tweaking and editing ad nauseum. The categories to have on your site include:

Work – You can make subcategories if you have a diverse portfolio.

Events – List any past events or upcoming events to demonstrate your scope of activity.

Media – Include this section if you have any encouraging press coverage you can share.

About – You can decide if you want to include a headshot or not. Either way is fine. For your bio, write a concise, insightful statement about why you do the work you do. Do not include personally identifying information such as the name of the school you attend, what town you live in, or any other information that you don't want strangers to know.

Contact – Protect your personal privacy. People should only be able to contact you through an online form, with a CAPTCHA or "I'm not a bot" verification step. Do not share your email, phone, address, or any other personal information on your site.

Website Hosting

I'm partial to using Wix.com for hosting and building websites as their tools are easy to use and have a lot of customization options. Wordpress.com is also popular. There are many options out there to choose from.

How to Make your Deliverables Look, Sound, and Feel Better

It's important that any deliverable you produce comes across as professional to adult audiences. When you envision what you want the final products of your work to like, you should strive for magazine-quality, book-quality, or even Netflix-quality production standards, which in general is worlds different that, say, Tik Tok or Facebook posting standards of production.

Here are some resources I've used successfully for stock photos, videos, and graphics; stock audio; illustrators; desktop publishing; and printing services.

Stock image resources

I'm a visual thinker so when I work with students on preparing their work for release, we tend to create visually impressive pieces, whatever the deliverable. When appropriate (which is often) we will include relevant, high-quality photos, illustrations, graphics, and icons that we've acquired from stock photo websites. It's amazing what even one really good image can have on a report or article, let alone several. Here are some of the resources we use:

Unsplash.com – (www.unsplash.com) royalty-free photos

Pexels.com – (www.pexels.com) royalty-free photos and videos

Pixabay.com – (www.pixabay.com) royalty-free photos, vector graphics, illustrations, videos, audio, and GIFs

Adobe Stock – (stock.adobe.com) This paid stock site has an enormous amount of high-quality content including photos, vectors, illustrations, videos, and audio. Their stock audio catalog is extensive, easily searchable, and I've often used it for background music in videos. Adobe requires you to purchase either a subscription or credit packages. I tend to find what I'm searching for faster and more efficiently on this paid site than I do on the free sites.

Custom illustrations

Fiverr.com – (www.fiverr.com) If you want to find someone with experience, consider posting a project request on Fiverr.com where you can hire a freelancer to design visuals for you at a moderate price.

DALL-E 2 – (openai.com/dall-e-2) Alternatively, you can try using AI-generated artwork from sites such as DALL-E 2.

Desktop publishing

Adobe InDesign – This is the industry-standard publishing app and is worth learning to use if you want to make professional-quality page layouts (for both print and digital). You can create pages of all types that go well beyond your best PowerPoint, Prezi, Word, or PhotoShop layouts. Templates are available (both free and premium) that can achieve the look and feel of high-quality magazines, brochures, posters, and other layouts. InDesign is part of Adobe Creative Cloud.

Printing resources

If you need to create high-quality printed materials for your projects, two resources to be aware of are Docucopies and PrintNinja. Of course, you can always use your local overnight printer but when time permits (to allow for production time and shipping), printers such as these two offer more options and paper types, which may allow you to create a more customized product for your needs.

Docucopies.com – (www.docucopies.com) I use this printer on a regular basis for their wide range of products, paper choices, and reasonably economical pricing. They have been helpful in reviewing my project's production files to ensure are acceptable for printing properly.

PrintNinja.com – (www.printninja.com) In addition to the typical print services of most printers, for $5 PrintNinja will send you a paper sample kit containing a complete selection of papers so you can feel the weight, finish, coating, and tactile feel of different papers, if that's going to be important to your project. They sell sample kits for books, cards, packaging, board games, and custom pieces. You can purchase the sample books without requiring placing a custom print order.

Chapter 13 – Develop Your Personal Brand

In our hyper-connected world, where the line separating our private lives and public-facing lives continue to thin, it's more important than ever for serious applicants to curate their outward-facing image while shielding their private lives from the general public. Developing your personal brand also forces you to decide what, in essence, is your essence. What do you want people to recognize you as or associate you with? What do you want to lead with?

Think like a movie star who has a good public relations team. They are careful to post online only those photos, videos, and messages that present them in some admirable light. All the mundane, sloppy, unfiltered personal information is kept hidden to protect their privacy, mental health, and safety.

Be fully aware that college admissions teams scan applicants' social media and online profiles. It can make or break a decision. And tracking down your social media accounts through your email addresses or other personal information is extremely easy for colleges to do using paid services.

Given that admissions teams are looking for reasons to say "No" more than "Yes," realize that your social media posts from Friday night parties are not as witty or clever as you think they are, at least not to overworked admissions officers. We'll discuss specific steps to wipe out any potentially negative information in your social media as well as promote more appealing content to craft your public persona.

Understand how colleges stalk you

Student data for sale

Colleges and universities can place enormous time, energy, and resources into crafting their reputations as world-class institutions. The makeup of their student body and the ease or difficulty of gaining acceptance are key elements in an institution's perceived desirability and ranking on influential lists such as the overly influential *U.S. News & World Report* Best Colleges Ranking. Many institutions employ sophisticated targeting and marketing strategies to attract large numbers of applicants, assess prospective candidates on different desirability traits, and increase the institution's branding as a highly-desirable school.

According to a November 5, 2019 *Wall Street Journal* article[9], many of the nation's top schools license hundreds of thousands of high school student's names and data from the College Board, the not-for-profit organization that administers the SAT and Advanced Placement exams, which generated $1.1 billion in revenues

---

[9] Douglas Belkin, "For Sale: SAT-Takers' Names. Colleges Buy Student Data and Boost Exclusivity," *The Wall Street Journal*, n.d., https://www.wsj.com/articles/for-sale-sat-takers-names-colleges-buy-student-data-and-boost-exclusivity-11572976621.

in 2019.[10] The College Board licenses information including students' names, ethnicities, PSAT and SAT scores, and the level of education their parents achieved. At a cost of about 47 cents per student, a college might license student information through the College Board's Student Search Service. The college can then create its own lists based on specific student characteristics, and then target students on those lists for "recruitment." Targeted students are often sent promotional material from the college encouraging them to apply. The vast majority of students end up getting rejected. But for the school, the strategy can be valuable: By increasing the number of applicants, it artificially drives down the colleges' overall admissions rate, making them seem more exclusive in the eyes of parents and applicants.

In its report, the Journal focused on Vanderbilt University in Nashville, Tennessee, which had an acceptance rate of 11 percent in 2017. By comparison, 17 years ago, the school had a generous acceptance rate of 46 percent. Other universities across the country have seen their admission rates drastically shrink in the past two decades. The licensing of student data may inflate the number of applicants even further. Colleges buy lists that combine different student variables together to create lists of targetable recruits, according to the *Journal*.[11]

Students taking the SAT typically check a box that asks them if they want to share their personal information with schools. They're led to believe that sharing their personal data may help them get recruited by the school but the chances of that actually happening are exceedingly low, according to the *Journal*. Test-takers — who may spend significant amounts of money on test prep and the test itself — are having their own data sold without any apparent benefit to themselves.[12]

College websites are watching your clicks

Colleges are using some of the same marketing tools that companies use to follow their customers through the sales funnel, in this case it's about getting attractive candidates from the application process to acceptance to enrollment.

The pinpoint accuracy of data-driven marketing might shove aside traditional name-buying among colleges as admissions officials become more conscious of the cost of purchasing tens of thousands of names that result in enrolled students. Data analysis companies are able to track the manner in which prospective students engage with college websites. A college has a number of ways of identifying who might be viewing their website, including when a candidate creates an online account with their basic information, subscribing to newsletters, or by sending prospective candidates customized links to their website. Website

---

[10] "College Entrance Examination Board - GuideStar Profile," Guidestar, https://www.guidestar.org/profile/13-1623965.

[11] Belkin, "For Sale: SAT-Takers' Names. Colleges Buy Student Data and Boost Exclusivity."

[12] Mack DeGeurin, "The College Board Is Licensing the Personal Data of Students Taking the SAT to Colleges so They Can Reject More Students and Inflate Admissions Numbers," Insider, https://www.insider.com/college-board-sat-student-data-colleges-to-reject-students-admissions-2019-11.

capturing software can monitor and record a visitor's activities, including the frequency of visits and time spent on different pages such as athletics or financial aid.

According to an April 11, 2017 article by *The Atlantic*, using that data, admissions officers can better understand the digital breadcrumbs students follow during the college search process, particularly what they do before they decide to apply or enroll. This type of data-mining, provided by marketing firms such as Kentucky-based Capture Higher Ed, enables schools to more narrowly target messaging or send personalized content to specific candidates.[13] Colleges can also infer if a candidate is likely to request financial aid based on the amount of time spent on those pages, which conceivably could be further corroborated by additional data mining into the candidate's parents.

Before you apply, clean your social media

In the realm of competitive college admissions, reviewing an applicant's social media allows schools to gain a more holistic perspective on a candidate. A 2018 Kaplan Test Prep survey found that about 25 percent of college admissions officers review applicants' social media profiles.

According to an August 22, 2019 *U.S. News & World Report* article, in a 2017 survey administered by the American Association of Collegiate Registrars and Admissions Officers, 11 percent of respondents said they "denied [a candidate's] admission based on social media content" and another 7 percent rescinded offers for the same reason.[14]

Before you hit "Submit" on your college (or even high school) applications, consider doing the following to ensure your social media footprint puts your best foot forward:

1. Your username says a lot about you, so choose something that presents you accurately and professionally.

2. Search for yourself online. A Google search for your name (and any variations you might use) may find pictures, profiles, and comments that may not be additive to the persona you want to present. Determine if anything out there should be deleted, edited, or refined.

3. Check the privacy settings on all your social media accounts. Depending on your activity on a particular platform or chatroom,

---

[13] Jeffrey Selingo, "Colleges Are Tracking Prospective Students' Digital Footprints," The Atlantic, April 11, 2017, https://www.theatlantic.com/education/archive/2017/04/how-colleges-find-their-students/522516/.

[14] John Moody, "Why Colleges Look at Students' Social Media Accounts | Best Colleges | US News," U.S. News & World Report, https://www.usnews.com/education/best-colleges/articles/2019-08-22/why-colleges-look-at-students-social-media-accounts.

you may want to limit the visibility of content to viewers whom you do not know.

4. Scan your 'Lists'. Depending on the platform, this may be your 'Likes' or 'Interests' on Facebook or those you are listed as 'Following' on Twitter or Instagram. These are your assumed interests, so make sure they are reasonably aligned with what you consider your college and professional goals.

5. Check your photos! Carefully review the images on all social media to ensure there are no inappropriate and irrelevant images that might hurt your candidacy. This includes images containing mature content, nudity, alcohol, drugs, offensive language or signs.[15]

At a minimum, set all accounts to Private

If you're not ready or not willing (gasp!) to create separate public and private accounts, at least set your existing social media accounts to Private, where followers must request permission to view your posts.

Along with doing this, take a look at your existing connections and determine if there are any random followers or outsiders who should be removed from seeing your posts and remove them.

Furthermore, it would be a healthy habit to go back through your existing postings and see if there is anything that would be prudent to delete for posterity. You decide if that is worthwhile.

Below are instructions on how to change the privacy settings of several social media sites. Other sites not included below likely have similar steps to change your settings. In general, it's best to allow only your friends, and friends of friends if you choose, to see your personal pages.

Note: Different site and apps may use either ••• or ⋮ or ≡ or some other symbol for the More Options menu. For purposes of simplicity in this guide, we'll be using ••• (called an ellipsis) as the general symbol for selecting the More Options menu, but it may vary with the above symbols depending on your computer or mobile device.

---

[15] Michael James Huss, "Do Colleges Look at Your Social Media?," https://admissions.usf.edu/blog/do-colleges-look-at-your-social-media.

Facebook privacy settings

1. Only allow Friends of Friends to connect with you, not Everyone.
2. Set your privacy to reduce how people can look you up, by email or phone.
3. Restrict search engines from finding your timeline.
4. Turn off the option for people to review your past posts.
5. Check the setting requiring your permission before friends tag you in photos.
6. Block people who are not beneficial to your wellbeing.
7. Change settings to require your approval when Friends tag you in posts

Instagram privacy settings

1. Personal Instagram accounts can be set to either Public or Private. When someone wants to follow a Private account, they must first send a request to the account owner, who can either approve or deny their access.
2. Keep in mind that a Private account sharing on other social media, such as Twitter, may make their Instagram-private post visible on a public Twitter account.
3. If someone was already following you before you set your Instagram posts to Private and you don't want them to see your posts, you can block them.
4. People can still send a photo or video directly to you even if they're not following you.

Snapchat privacy settings

1. On the Camera screen, tap your profile icon at the top
2. Tap ⚙ to open **Settings**
3. Scroll down to the **Who Can…** section and tap **Contact Me**
4. Choose **My Friends** to make it so only your friends will be able to Snap and Chat you
5. Tap the **Back** button to update your privacy settings.

TikTok privacy settings

To make your TikTok private, tap the ••• in the upper right portion of the screen, and then navigate to **Privacy and Safety** and change your settings.

Twitter privacy settings

      To make your tweets private, go to **Privacy and safety settings** and check **Protect my Tweets**.

Even better, create a 2nd account and don't cross-fertilize

      If you're going to be active online, consider your existing account to be your public account, and create a second account for your closest friends and relationships. Importantly, when you set up your account, use a separate email that is not easily identified as being owned by you, meaning don't use your actual name in the address or account setup. While many services are trying to move toward requiring actual and true names, there is still a lot of leeway to be creative.

      If your true name is, say, Regina Smith, your new social media account name should be something unrelated or connected to you and your life. "AmericanCheez52" or "Boston Beans" are perfectly acceptable user and account names, or whatever you fancy. Once you set up your new accounts, determine who you want to be connected to privately and – importantly –delete those connections from your public account. You do not want to cross-contaminate accounts with shared users because determined threat actors will often research a target's followers or connections to gather information. If a threat actor can only find your carefully-curated -public account (which you will diligently ensure never reveals important personal information, right?) then you have created a buffer of protection. By not allowing users to follow both of your accounts, you are compartmentalizing yourself, which is valuable to preserving and maintaining your privacy.

Don't use Google, Facebook or automatic logins for other sites

      Nowadays, when creating a new user account, many sites and apps will give you the option of signing in using your Google, Facebook, Twitter or other accounts. We will call these "primary" accounts for clarification here, and the non-Google, non-Facebook, non-Twitter accounts are "subaccounts" for this discussion. While using primary accounts to log into subaccounts is much easier and tempting because doing so doesn't require you to type in your basic info or creating another password, we recommend against doing so.

      This "convenience" is not for your benefit, it's so Google and Facebook can monitor your activities even more than they are already through cross-collection of information. Always create separate accounts with separate passwords.

      Another downside to this convenience is that if someone gains access to that primary account, they then have access to all of the shared accounts. What's more, all the stalker or scammer needs to do is check the messages or permissions in the primary account to see which other accounts have been granted sharing permission for a roadmap to your digital life.

It's also easy enough for hackers to create illegitimate websites that allow you to log in with your primary accounts, and the scammer just obtained your primary account's actual username and password.

Although it takes just a few more steps in the beginning setup process, create unique usernames and passwords for all of your accounts.

Chapter 14 – Learn how to Tell Your Story

Okay, this one is hard, I'll admit it. High schoolers are mostly taught how to write book reports, which don't necessarily need to be interesting, just written according to a points-based rubric (which makes words on the page even less engaging).

When your application essays are strictly limited to 250, 500, or 650 words (or somewhere in between) every word counts. Now with AI ensuring most (if not all) essays are going to be written exceptionally well, your ability to show evidence of your capabilities is even more vital. But you should still know how to write well.

AI is completely rewriting the Ivy League college admissions game.

"When everyone's super, no one will be."

In the animated movie The Incredibles, the villain Syndrome plots to sell his Iron Man-quality tech to the public, so anyone – on the surface – can look like a superhero. It's an allegory (good SAT word by the way) for what AI is doing to today's elite college admissions landscape, where hundreds of thousands of young adults compete desperately for acceptance letters.

In years past, writing an outstanding Common App essay and excellent supplemental essays were an essential component of a solid application. There used to be value in the craft of writing, whether the applicant's topic was growing up under adversity, pursuing their "passion" (a grossly overused application term), or even what, on an existential level, chocolate chip cookies or boba drinks meant to them. Good writing used to be an indication of a high school student's maturity, capabilities, and perspective, which used to be materially additive to the quality of their application.

Colleges may state that applicants are not allowed to use ChatGPT or other AI tools, but it's happening nevertheless. Whether it's merely having AI structure an essay outline or craft an entire piece of prose worthy of Ernest Hemingway (you can literally prompt AI to "write like Hemingway would write"), it's safe to assume the overall quality of college essays is going to skyrocket. Going forward, every candidate will be able to present a masterful narrative about themselves.

Don't believe me? Adults are already doing the same on LinkedIn. Scroll through the "About" section of, say, 10 or 20 of your random contacts and you'll likely notice how many people are self-described experts, visionaries, thought leaders, award-winners, and otherwise brilliant, shining personalities. I'm not saying they're not, but on the LinkedIn everyone is super.

In years past, my work with clients focused heavily on helping each candidate figuring out what their individual narrative was, how they could tell their story in a way nobody else could. As a journalist, I have a love for words so there was always an intellectual gratification reading a student's first-rate essay writing, knowing it came from both their heart and brain. Nowadays, any student who can write an effective AI prompt will crank out the same quality in minutes rather than months.

So what's a hardworking student to do today to get into Harvard, Princeton, or Stanford tomorrow? Now more than ever, it's important to show, don't tell. Talk is cheap, so points on the proverbial board matter. Contenders will have to show accomplishments that stand on their own in the "grown up" world, preferably with accompanying URL links or deliverables as proof. I always advise my clients not to explain in an application why or how their work is important or impressive, but rather simply present the information in plain, unembellished English and let the reviewer decide for themselves if an accomplishment has merit, which is a much more powerful way to build credibility.

Our Manual of Style

Avoid and eschew unnecessarily descriptive scene-setting embellishment and overly-lengthy extended word-consuming verbosity

"Heart pounding, hands shaking, I stepped out onto the blinding stage for the first time…."

"The stifling tropical air hit me full on as I stepped off the plane…"

"The sweat dripped from my brow as I raced to complete my paper by the midnight deadline…"

"As I surveyed the empty test tubes standing at attention in the rack on my table, I laid out my test samples in an orderly line, generals waiting to address their soldiers…"

I find these openers tiresome and time consuming. In isolation these would be fine as essays, but when they are added to an assembly line of applications to review, there's likely little that hasn't already been described in flowery prose by someone else before, thus in a crowd I don't find these types of descriptions memorable. Sometimes it is helpful to set a scene, but the scene must be distinct enough and significant enough to merit the sendup. Everyone has, at some point, stepped onto a stage or public space so we all know that sort of feeling. Not so interesting. Stepping into outer space or 200 feet below the ocean's surface or the UN General Assembly podium? That can grab my attention. Stepping somewhere in between those extreme examples? Maybe, but do be picky on what is worth writing about.

Topics to avoid*

Sports as a metaphor for life – *"slowly but surely through my continued efforts I grew more confident as my skills increased, leading up to the final game where I..."* There are only so many sports in the world, and they've all be written about, even pickleball.

Parents getting divorced – While this subject is highly personal, it's happened elsewhere and often, so it is exceptionally hard to be memorable. Being raised by a single parent? That has some potential for an element in your larger narrative but is has to be out of the ordinary.

One or both parents dying while the student was very young – Please accept my deep condolences. For the purposes of the essays this topic is used a lot. It might be additive as an arc element, but typically should not be the main focus of an essay, unless that loss is spurring you to seek a cure, seek justice, seek peace, or seek revenge.

Skydiving – Yes it's exhilarating, Yes you stepped out of your comfort zone, but you were most likely strapped to a trained professional. You got to wear a cool jumpsuit and goggles, but realistically gravity did most of the work. If you ended up skydiving unintentionally (e.g., Action Movie tropes), or your first parachute failed and for a moment you truly contemplated the meaning of life waiting for your reserve chute to open, or are a Certified Jump Master, then you are allowed to use it in an essay, assuming you lived to write about it.

* Topics to avoid except when there is something truly distinctive in the story such as: you almost died in the process, you saved someone's life in the process, your actions uncovered a major injustice and justice was ultimately delivered, or your actions impacted tens, hundreds, or thousands of lives in a positive, lasting, and measurable manner.

Words and phrases to avoid

"in order to" – is the same as "to". "In order to overcome…" is the same as "To overcome…" but it takes 3 words instead of just 1 word. Brevity is important in all writing.

"There is," "There was," "There are," "There were" and so on – using "there" in this manner is telling about something, not showing. "There was an angry buffalo chasing me" is not as interesting as "An angry buffalo chased me."

Unique – Describing something as unique does not describe anything at all. Saying something is unique means you don't know how to explain what you're talking about to the reader. Try harder to be illustrative.

Utilize – Use "use" instead of the word "utilize." "Utilize" is just a long, unnecessary way to say use, and people often use it when trying make what they are doing sound overly important or complex but instead it just adds verbosity, which is to be avoided. Use use.

Very – Once you finish writing your essay, do a word search for the word "very" and delete it everywhere it appears. Very is a very weak word, use a better description for whatever it is you are discussing. Deleting very also makes space in your available word count. [I did the same for this book. No *very*s anywhere except this paragraph.]

Wordplay

Done right, the ability to play with words keeps writing fresh for the reader and enjoyable for the writer (sometimes). Playing with words – wordplay – means using words or phrases in ways that that are divergent or unexpected. It's an art, not a science. A reader will sense if it's forced writing or free-flowing wit, whether the writer is trying hard to sound clever or inherently having fun as they type on their keyboard. It's a high hurdle.

One example of strong wordplay comes from Bono, the lead singer of the band U2, in his autobiography *Surrender*. As a songwriter and lyricist, his grasp of language and ability to use tone and tenor effectively in his personal narrative was refreshing in parts, even fun to read. Take a read if you can before writing your essays. If you can't before deadline, add it to your reading list anyway to hone your craft.

Writing habits to develop

Do the *New York Times* crossword puzzle regularly

Over time, the *New York Times* crossword presents opportunity to grow your vocabulary, broaden your cultural knowledge, and – most importantly – learn how words and definitions can be reinterpreted and played with. It's free online and on their app. It's a slow, slow process but I find it both valuable and satisfying in my lifelong learning journey. While there are countless crossword providers out there, the *New York Times* is compelling because the puzzles increase in difficulty as the days go on. The Monday crossword is the easiest and they get progressively harder until the most challenging Saturday puzzle. The Sunday puzzle is a larger, medium-difficulty puzzle, so it takes more time but is not the most challenging. Given the difficulty scale, you can easily measure your personal progress based on how far you get on any given day. Crushing the Monday puzzles but getting nowhere far on Wednesdays? Rinse and repeat. Increment by increment you can build your mental database and experience archives of how letters, words, and phrases can be stretched, smushed, smashed, and smoothed into new meanings. Your readers and listeners will thank you for it.

Audiobooks

I've said before that time is either invested or spent. If the opportunity presents itself, such as while commuting, driving, exercising, or other tasks where you can multitask efficiently, consider listening to audiobooks instead of music. I appreciate that music nourishes your soul from time to time and is important; however, paying attention to writing – both good and bad writing – can both educate you and provide references and examples of how you can make your own voice and writing resonate. The same way a good chef should have tasted many different cuisines, a good writer should have exposure to a diverse range of genres, styles, and authors. Make the effort to actively listen, imagine what the author's process and objective was as they crafted their sentences. Think about how fluid and seamless or clunky and forced are the images that form in your mind as you hear the narration.

As you write your essays (and anything else for that matter) keep in mind how your word choice and sentences will sound in the reader's head. Keep it clear, keep it interesting, and keep it concise.

Chapter 15 – Practice Frequent Self-Care

Let's be honest, the college application process sucks. It blows. It's artificial pressure on you to keep up with the fast-moving pack of hundreds of thousands of people your age to move on to a next major stage of your life.

I said previously that I'll speak to you like an adult, so do understand that I don't want you to devote yourself to the strategies in this book at the expense of your genuine well-being. I am perfectly happy to push you do to things that are well outside your comfort zone – even encourage you to do things that are intimidating and exhausting – but only within the boundaries of your best judgement. Just as in all aspects of life, know when to say "When."

You are likely experiencing a whirlwind of academic pressures, social challenges, and personal growth situations. Amid all the demands swirling around you, it is essential to remember that your mental health is the key to thriving during this transformative period. Self-care is the opposite of self-harm, and it's important for you to determine which side you want for yourself. I'll be sharing information and recommendations for you to consider to care for what truly matters: **You**.

Mental Health is the cornerstone of well-being

Before we talk about healthy strategies, it's crucial to grasp the concept of mental health. It encompasses your emotional, psychological, and social well-being, affecting how you think, feel, and act. In essence, mental health serves as the cornerstone for a balanced and fulfilling life. Mental health is more than the absence of mental disorders. It exists on a complex continuum, which is experienced differently from one person to the next, with varying degrees of difficulty and distress and potentially very different social and clinical outcomes.[16]

Find Your Calm

Mindfulness is a state of active, open attention to the present and observing your thoughts and feelings without judging them as good or bad. To live mindfully is to live in the moment and reawaken oneself to the present, rather than dwelling on the past or anticipating the future – essentially being "in the moment" and appreciating the ride (or roller coaster) you are on. To be mindful is to observe and label thoughts, feelings, and sensations in the body in an objective manner. Being

---

[16] "Mental Health," World Health Organization, n.d., https://www.who.int/news-room/fact-sheets/detail/mental-health-strengthening-our-response.

mindful can help you avoid self-criticism and judgment while identifying and managing difficult emotions.[17]

Unplug yourself

In today's hyperconnected world, taking time for yourself is vital for mental rejuvenation. Step away from screens, social media, and distractions, and engage in activities that bring you joy and introspection. Whether it's journaling, reading, or spending time in nature, "me-time" helps you recharge and reduce stress.

Americans spend a daily average of four hours watching TV and about seven-and-a-half hours on digital devices. Unsurprisingly, so much screen time is stressing many of us out. The solution may be a digital detox, which can provide relief from the pressures of constant connection to electronic devices. Research has found that doing a digital detox may even help improve your sleep, relationships and mood. Taking a break from viewing or engaging in social media is the most popular form of a digital detox. Negative social media experiences can trigger anxiety and depression and affect self-esteem. This includes:

- Being angry or upset over posted content;
- Cyberbullying (online verbal bullying);
- Fear of missing out (FOMO);
- Feelings of isolation; and
- Social comparisons.

The results of unplugging can be far reaching, from being more productive to deepening your relationships with family and friends. During a digital detox, you may find that you notice more in your immediate surroundings. Your brain can concentrate much better on your tasks. Eliminating digital distractions creates more opportunities to pay attention to those around you. On average, Americans check their smartphones 96 times a day and spend more than two hours on social media. For many people, checking their phone or social media whenever there's a few free minutes is a reflex action that is not based on any real need. Taking a break from digital devices or media helps you combat compulsive use.

Practice Effective Time Management

With various classes and assignments, time management becomes your ally. Create a study schedule, set realistic goals, and prioritize tasks to strike a balance between academics and self-care. Effective time management reduces stress and increases productivity.

---

[17] "Mindfulness," Psychology Today, n.d., https://www.psychologytoday.com/us/basics/mindfulness.

Prioritize Quality Sleep

Sleep is not a luxury but a necessity for your mental health. Aim for eight to ten hours of quality sleep each night to ensure your brain and body receive the rest they need. Adequate sleep boosts mood, cognitive function, and overall well-being. Do everything in your power to make sleep a priority in your schedule. This means budgeting for the hours you need so that work or social activities do not trade off with sleep. While cutting sleep short may be tempting in the moment, it does not pay off in the long run because sleep is essential for you to perform at your best, both mentally and physically. Getting more sleep is a key part of the equation, but remember that it is not just about sleep quantity. Quality sleep matters too, and it is possible to get the hours that you need but not feel refreshed because your sleep is fragmented or non-restorative. Worship your bed.[18]

Release Endorphins, Reduce Stress

Exercise is a potent stress reducer that benefits both your physical and mental health. When you engage in physical activity, your body releases endorphins – natural mood enhancers that promote positive feelings and reduce stress. Find an activity you enjoy, whether it's dancing, sports, yoga, or even playing Beat Saber on your VR headset and incorporate it into your routine.[19]

Lean on Your Support System: You Are Not Alone

High school can be a maze of challenges, but remember that you don't have to navigate it alone. Reach out to friends, family, teachers, or school counselors when you need support. Sharing your thoughts and emotions can alleviate stress and provide valuable guidance.

---

[18] "How Much Sleep Do We Really Need?," Sleep Foundation, March 9, 2021, https://www.sleepfoundation.org/how-sleep-works/how-much-sleep-do-we-really-need.

[19] "Exercise Is an All-Natural Treatment to Fight Depression," Harvard Health, July 17, 2013, https://www.health.harvard.edu/mind-and-mood/exercise-is-an-all-natural-treatment-to-fight-depression.

Seek Support: Reach Out When Needed

Seeking help is a sign of strength and shows your commitment to learning and growth. When pressures mount, don't hesitate to seek support. Teachers, academic advisors, family, friends, and peers can provide guidance and assistance to help you navigate difficult situations or issues. If you find yourself struggling with overwhelming emotions or stress, reach out to a mental health professional. They are trained to provide tailored support to help you navigate through challenging times. You'll thank yourself later.

Strengthen your self-awareness

Self-awareness is having a clear understanding of your strengths, limitations, emotions, beliefs, and motivations. It sounds simple enough, but most people don't do this completely. In an October 23, 2019 *Harvard Business School* article, 79 percent of business executives surveyed by the organizational consulting firm Korn Ferry had at least one blind spot – or a skill they ranked among their strongest that others reported as a weakness. For that 79 percent, their self-awareness was not as objective as they perceived it to be. By acknowledging your own strengths and (current) weaknesses, you can be better equipped to make more thoughtful decisions about the things that will benefit and protect you.

Understand self-regulation

Self-regulation refers to how you manage your emotions, behaviors, and impulses. The more self-aware you are, the easier this becomes; if you can recognize what you're feeling and why, you can respond appropriately. If you are prone to mood swings, emotional outbursts or overreacting, there are tactics you can use to improve your self-regulation, such as:

Pause Before Responding – Give yourself time to stop and think before immediately replying. This could be as simple as taking a deep breath and allowing for a 20-second pause so that your feelings get out of the way of your thoughts.

Take a Step Back – Sometimes, you might need to leave the room, and that's okay. It's often better to take a walk, drink some water, or call a friend than to make a snap judgment or decision that you'll regret later.

Recognize Your Emotions – Try logging or making note of what it is you're feeling and what is causing you stress. You'll likely start identifying patterns. If you know what triggers you, the next time a similar situation occurs, you'll be better positioned to handle it in a healthy, positive way.

If you acknowledge your emotions and give yourself time to process them, you can carefully craft how you respond and keep yourself pointed in the direction you want to go.[20]

Embrace a Growth Mindset

Developing a growth mindset empowers you to view challenges as stepping stones for growth and improvement. Embrace setbacks as opportunities to learn and develop, knowing that perseverance and effort lead to success.

Prioritizing mental health and managing stress are fundamental for a successful and fulfilling journey at every stage of our lives. By incorporating self-care strategies, controlling academic stress (as opposed to letting it control you), and appreciating your own emotional resilience, you can equip yourself with the tools to thrive in high school and beyond.

Remember, you matter. Your mental well-being matters too, and by nurturing it you can confidently face any challenge that comes your way. You are worthy of it and you deserve it.

---

[20] "How to Develop Emotional Intelligence Skills," Harvard Business School Online: Business Insights Blog, October 23, 2019, https://online.hbs.edu/blog/post/emotional-intelligence-skills.

Epilogue

Now that we've discussed all the philosophies, tactics, techniques, and procedures of what it takes to be accepted into Ivy League and other top colleges and universities, here is the lasting message I want to impart to you:

Think bigger than college. If you have invested in yourself by executing on the strategies in this book, it does not matter where you go to college because you are bigger and of greater worth than any school's name.

Read that again. I'm serious.

I already said in the first sentence of the first chapter to think bigger than college, remember? That's what we've been working toward throughout this book. Whether or not you will succeed in any school environment is 100 percent up to you. You have the agency to decide how "successful" (whatever that means to you) you will be, wherever you spend your four years. I have said all along that our goal together is to make you bigger than high school, even bigger than college. And that's the intrinsic value we seek to achieve. No single college can empower you or prevent you from achieving your personal greatness. Do I believe these strategies will make you highly attractive to the institutions that should be able to recognize your worth? Absolutely Yes. If a faceless admissions committee fails to see that and – for whatever reason – declines your application, fuck it. No hard feelings and no regrets on your part.

Perhaps it will be their loss or perhaps they won't even notice your absence. That is out of your control and that is fine. Your job, for the rest of your life, is to direct yourself on your own terms as much as possible, raising yourself and those around you up every step of the way.

Confidence often comes with competence, and through our journey together I sincerely hope you are recognizing the strengths and capabilities you continue to hone. Remember, you want to be a pull, not a push. A great Indy 500 racecar driver may be a disastrous NASCAR, Monaco Grand Prix, or Le Mans driver and vice versa yet each of those worlds have their individual merits. The same goes for colleges and universities. The greatest gift you have is your personal agency to decide and direct how you can thrive going forward. No institution or committee or even family or friend can decide that for you, no matter how much they might want to. You are your own driver.

Vroom vroom.

– Daniel Farber Huang

APPENDIX

Prospective Media Outlets for Articles

The below list includes numerous major print and online media outlets that accept freelance submissions. More information on each outlet's submission guidelines can be found in the links. Note that some publications require pitches being sent to them to be exclusive, meaning the pitch is not simultaneously being sent to other publications at the same time.

#	Publication	Category	Genre	Website
1.	Asbury Park Press	Op-ed, Editorial	General	https://static.usatoday.com/submitcolumn/
2.	Atlantic, The	Editorial, Fiction, Poetry	General	https://support.theatlantic.com/hc/en-us/articles/360011374734-Submit-a-piece-for-editorial-consideration-at-The-Atlantic
3.	Baltimore Sun	Op-ed, Editorial	General	https://www.baltimoresun.com/opinion/bal-oped-submission-ngux-htmlstory.html
4.	Bon Appetit	Varied	Lifestyle	https://www.bonappetit.com/story/how-to-pitch
5.	Boston Globe	Op-ed	General	https://www.bostonglobe.com/2019/12/26/opinion/submit-an-op-ed/
6.	Boston Herald	Letters to the Editor	General	https://www.bostonherald.com/contact-us/
7.	Business Insider	Op-ed, Editorial	Business	https://www.businessinsider.com/how-to-write-for-business-insider-2020-4
8.	Bustle Magazine	Op-ed, Editorial	Women	https://www.bustle.com/p/how-to-submit-freelance-pitches-to-bustle-11914601
9.	Buzzfeed	Op-ed, Editorial	General	https://www.buzzfeednews.com/article/rachelysanders/how-to-pitch-essays-to-buzzfeed-reader
10.	Chicago Tribune	Op-ed	General	https://www.chicagotribune.com/opinion/commentary/chi-opedguidelines-story-story.html

11.	**Cosmopolitan Magazine UK**	Op-ed	Women	https://www.cosmopolitan.com/uk/worklife/careers/a25425/write-for-cosmopolitan/
12.	**Cosmos**	Varied, Photography	Science and Tech	https://cosmosmagazine.com/submissions/
13.	**DAME Magazine**	Op-ed, Editorial	Women	https://www.damemagazine.com/about/
14.	**Discover**	Varied	Science and Tech	https://www.discovermagazine.com/pitch-guide
15.	**Economist**	Varied	Business	https://www.economist.com/1843/2021/08/15/pitching-guidelines
16.	**Fast Company**	Business topics	Business	https://www.fastcompany.com/3008467/guidelines-submitting-contributed-articles-fast-company-and-tips-getting-published
17.	**Financial Times**	Op-ed, Editorial	Business	https://www.ft.com/content/e3e8ff2b-95c7-48f8-9eda-312494422e10
18.	**Fortune**	Business topics	Business	https://fortune.com/2021/04/15/how-to-pitch-fortune-get-a-story-picked-up-business-magazine-freelance-work-pitching-advice/
19.	**Huffington Post**	Op-ed	General	https://www.huffpost.com/static/how-to-pitch-huffpost
20.	**Inc.**	Business topics	Business	https://www.inc.com/columnist-proposal-pitch-form.html
21.	**Insider**	Op-ed, Editorial	General	https://www.insider.com/how-to-write-for-insider-life-division
22.	**Intercept, The**	Op-ed, Editorial	General	https://theintercept.com/how-to-pitch-to-the-intercept/
23.	**Lifehacker**	General	General	https://lifehacker.com/about
24.	**Live Science**	Varied	Science and Tech	https://www.livescience.com/how-to-pitch-live-science

25.	**Los Angeles Times**	Op-ed	General	https://www.latimes.com/oe-howtosubmitoped-story.html
26.	**Men's Health UK**	Varied	Men	https://www.menshealth.com/uk/fitness/lifestyle/a37688513/pitch-to-mens-health/
27.	**Ms. Magazine**	Women's voices	Women	https://msmagazine.com/submissions/
28.	**National Geographic - social media photos**	Photography	General	https://www.instagram.com/natgeoyourshot/
29.	**NewScientist**	Varied	Science and Tech	https://www.newscientist.com/freelancers/
30.	**New York Daily News**	Op-ed, Editorial	General	https://www.nydailynews.com/opinion/submit-op-ed-daily-news-article-1.3802506
31.	**New York Magazine**	General	General	https://nymag.com/contactus/
32.	**New York Times**	Op-ed	General	https://help.nytimes.com/hc/en-us/sections/115003870867-Reader-Submissions
33.	**New Yorker**	Varied. Fiction, Poetry, Cartoons	General	https://www.newyorker.com/about/contact
34.	**Newark Star Ledger, Times of Trenton**	Op-ed	General	https://www.nj.com/opinion/2018/01/submit_an_op-ed.html
35.	**Newsday (NY)**	Op-ed	General	https://www.newsday.com/opinion/submit-your-letter-1.2516352
36.	**Philadelphia Inquirer**	Op-ed	General	https://www.inquirer.com/opinion/commentary/philadelphia-inquirer-op-ed-opinion-pitch-submission-20191129.html
37.	**PopSugar.com**	Women's voices	General	https://www.popsugar.com/Writing-POPSUGAR-40810428

38.	**Popular Mechanics**	Varied	General	https://www.popularmechanics.com/about/a34246962/how-to-pitch-popular-mechanics/
39.	**Popular Science**	Varied	Science and Tech	https://www.popsci.com/writers-guidelines/
40.	**Prism Reports**	Op-ed, Editorial	BIPOC	https://prismreports.org/about/call-for-pitches/
41.	**Providence Journal**	Op-ed	General	https://www.providencejournal.com/story/opinion/columns/2021/06/16/guidelines-submitting-letter-editor-column-providence-journal/5295892001/
42.	**Refinery29**	Op-ed	Women	https://www.refinery29.com/en-us/2014/04/66412/writing-for-r29
43.	**Root, The**	Op-ed	Black experience topics and perspectives	https://www.theroot.com/call-for-submissions-the-root-wants-your-story-1790876535
44.	**Scientific American**	Varied, Poetry	Science and Tech	https://www.scientificamerican.com/page/submission-instructions/
45.	**Science**	Varied	Science and Tech	https://www.science.org/content/page/science-information-authors
46.	**Shape**	Varied	Lifestyle	https://www.shape.com/about-us-5441927#toc-editorial-guidelines
47.	**Slate**	Op-ed, Editorial	General	https://slate.com/pitch
48.	**Smithsonian Magazine**	Varied	Science and Tech	https://www.smithsonianmag.com/contact/smithsonian-magazine-article-submissions/
49.	**Star Tribune (MN - 7th largest circulation)**	Op-ed	General	https://www.startribune.com/submit-a-letter-or-commentary/115289839/

50.	**TheScientist**	Varied	Science and Tech	https://www.the-scientist.com/freelance
51.	**Travel + Leisure**	Varied	Lifestyle	https://www.travelandleisure.com/travel-tips/how-to-pitch-travel-and-leisure
52.	**Undark.org**	Op-ed, Science	General	https://undark.org/submission-guidelines/
53.	**USA Today**	Op-ed	General	https://www.usatoday.com/story/opinion/2019/12/04/submit-letters-columns-and-comment-social/2608825001/
54.	**Vice**	Op-ed, Editorial	General	https://www.vice.com/en/article/m7ea7n/pitch-guidelines-for-the-vice-culture-desk
55.	**Wall Street Journal**	Op-ed	Business	https://www.wsj.com/articles/oped-guidelines-for-the-wall-street-journal-1384383173
56.	**Wanderful (Travel)**	Op-ed, Editorial	Lifestyle	https://sheswanderful.com/write/
57.	**Wired**	Op-ed	Science and Tech	https://www.wired.com/about/how-to-submit-to-wired-opinion/
58.	**Woman's Day**	Varied	Women	https://www.womansday.com/life/work-money/a56824/writers-guidelines/
59.	**Women's ENews Teen**	Women's voices	Women	https://womensenews.org/teen-voices/submission-guidelines/
60.	**Women's Health**	Varied	Women	https://www.womenshealthmag.com/about/a24170223/about-womens-health/
61.	**Women's Media Center - FBomb (Teen and College)**	Women's voices	Women	https://www.womensmediacenter.com/about/pitch-us

About the Author

Daniel Farber Huang is CEO of EchoStream Talent Group (www.echostreamgroup.com), which provides strategic talent management, personal branding, and bold mentorship to help clients transform potential into prominence and aspirations into achievements. Daniel is a former admissions reader for a top business school, having reviewed hundreds of applications from highly-qualified candidates. For years, he has advised and mentored high school clients on crafting distinctive, memorable, and successful applications for the most competitive colleges and universities both in the U.S. and globally.

He earned his Master's degree (A.L.M.) in Journalism and a Certificate in International Security from Harvard University, an M.B.A. from The Wharton School, University of Pennsylvania in Finance and Entrepreneurial Management, and a B.A. from New York University in Economics.

Bibliography

Belkin, Douglas. "For Sale: SAT-Takers' Names. Colleges Buy Student Data and Boost Exclusivity." *The Wall Street Journal*, https://www.wsj.com/articles/for-sale-sat-takers-names-colleges-buy-student-data-and-boost-exclusivity-11572976621.

Carlin, George. "Charlie Rose Interview - On Comedians Who Pick On The Underdogs." YouTube.com, https://www.youtube.com/watch?v=F8yV8xUorQ8.

DeGeurin, Mack. "The College Board Is Licensing the Personal Data of Students Taking the SAT to Colleges so They Can Reject More Students and Inflate Admissions Numbers." Insider, https://www.insider.com/college-board-sat-student-data-colleges-to-reject-students-admissions-2019-11.

Guidestar. "College Entrance Examination Board - GuideStar Profile," https://www.guidestar.org/profile/13-1623965.

Harvard Business School Online: Business Insights Blog. "How to Develop Emotional Intelligence Skills," October 23, 2019. https://online.hbs.edu/blog/post/emotional-intelligence-skills.

Harvard Health. "Exercise Is an All-Natural Treatment to Fight Depression," July 17, 2013. https://www.health.harvard.edu/mind-and-mood/exercise-is-an-all-natural-treatment-to-fight-depression.

Huss, Michael James. "Do Colleges Look at Your Social Media?" University of South Florida, https://admissions.usf.edu/blog/do-colleges-look-at-your-social-media.

Martin, Steve. "Charlie Rose Interview - Steve Martin." YouTube.com, https://www.youtube.com/watch?v=teAvv6jnuXY.

Mayo Clinic Health System. "3 Health Benefits of Volunteering," https://www.mayoclinichealthsystem.org/hometown-health/speaking-of-health/3-health-benefits-of-volunteering.

Moody, John. "Why Colleges Look at Students' Social Media Accounts." U.S. News & World Report, https://www.usnews.com/education/best-colleges/articles/2019-08-22/why-colleges-look-at-students-social-media-accounts.

Psychology Today. "Dunning-Kruger Effect," https://www.psychologytoday.com/us/basics/dunning-kruger-effect.

Psychology Today. "Mindfulness," https://www.psychologytoday.com/us/basics/mindfulness.

QuoteInvestigator.com. "Well-Behaved Women Seldom Make History," https://quoteinvestigator.com/2012/11/03/well-behaved-women/.

Rofe, Dr. J. Simon. "Understanding Research Methods - University of London." Coursera, https://www.coursera.org/learn/research-methods.

Selingo, Jeffrey. "Colleges Are Tracking Prospective Students' Digital Footprints." The Atlantic, April 11, 2017.

> https://www.theatlantic.com/education/archive/2017/04/how-colleges-find-their-students/522516/.

Sleep Foundation. "How Much Sleep Do We Really Need?," March 9, 2021. https://www.sleepfoundation.org/how-sleep-works/how-much-sleep-do-we-really-need.

"The OpEd Project," https://www.theopedproject.org/.

World Health Organization. "Mental Health," https://www.who.int/news-room/fact-sheets/detail/mental-health-strengthening-our-response.

www.ingramcontent.com/pod-product-compliance
Lightning Source LLC
Chambersburg PA
CBHW042358030426
42337CB00032B/5144